The WATCHMAKER'S DAUGHTER

Also by Sonia Taitz

Praise for *The Watchmaker's Daughter*

"A *heartbreaking memoir of healing power and redeeming devotion, Sonia Taitz's* The Watchmaker's Daughter *has the dovish beauty and levitating spirit of a psalm.* The suffering and endurance of Taitz's parents—Holocaust "death camp graduates" who met at the Lithuanian Jewish Survivors' Ball in a New York hotel (imagine Steven Spielberg photographing that dance-floor tableau)—form the shadow-hung backdrop of a childhood in a high-octane, postwar America where history seems weightless and tragedy a foreign import, a Hollywood paradise of perky blondes, Pepsodent smiles, and innocent high-school hijinks where our author and heroine longs to fit in. Although the wonder years that *Taitz scrupulously, tenderly, beautifully, often comically renders* aren't that far removed from us, they and the Washington Heights she grew up in, *the shop where her father repaired watches like a physician tending to the sick tick of time itself,* the grand movie houses where the image of Doris Day sunshined the giant screen, have acquired the ache and poignance of a lost, Kodachrome age. *A past is here reborn and tenderly restored with the love and absorption of a daughter with a final duty to perform a last act of fidelity.*"

—James Wolcott, *Vanity Fair* columnist
and author of *Lucking Out*

"Sonia Taitz's memoir of growing up the daughter of a master watch repairman who survived the Holocaust is also *a haunting meditation on time itself.* Taitz writes with *a painter's eye and a poet's voice.*"

—Mark Whitaker, author of *My Long Trip Home*

"Sonia Taitz's memoir of coming of age in postwar America is *unusually gentle, loving, and insightful.* This book's understanding of family dynamics and the realities of the American Dream will resonate with us all."
  —Joshua Halberstam, author of *A Seat at the Table*

"*Sonia Taitz captures time in this deeply moving memoir* of a woman's journey back to herself. *The Watchmaker's Daughter* is written with a wise eye and a generous heart. Unforgettable!"   —Christina Haag, author of *Come to the Edge*

Praise for *In the King's Arms*

"Beguiling . . . . Taitz zigzags among her culturally disparate characters, zooming in on their foibles with elegance and astringency."   —*The New York Times Book Review*

"In the province of gifted poets, playwrights and novelists."
  —*ForeWord Reviews*

"I thought often of Evelyn Waugh—the smart talk, the fey Brits, country houses, good clothes, lineage for centuries . . . Even the heavy moments have verve and wit."
  —Jesse Kornbluth, *Vanity Fair* essayist
  and editor of HeadButler.com

"In her gloriously rendered novel, *In the King's Arms*, Sonia Taitz writes passionately and wisely about outsiders, and what happens when worlds apart slam into each other."
  —Betsy Carter, author of
  The Puzzle King and *Nothing to Fall Back On*

The WATCHMAKER'S DAUGHTER

Sonia Taitz

McWitty Press   New York

Memory is by its nature imperfect, but with that caveat, all the events recounted in this memoir are true to the best of my recollection and recreative powers. In a few cases, most of them involving my own romantic history, names have been changed to protect the privacy of those concerned.

For information, address McWitty Press, 110 Riverside Drive,
New York, NY 10024.
www.mcwittypress.com

Cover design by Jennifer Carrow
Interior design by Abby Kagan

Library of Congress Control Number: 2012947484
ISBN: 978-0-9755618-8-1

Give me your tired, your poor,
Your huddled masses yearning to breathe free,
The wretched refuse of your teeming shore.
Send these, the homeless, tempest-tost, to me,
I lift my lamp beside the golden door!

EMMA LAZARUS
Inscription at base of the Statue of Liberty,
New York Harbor

To the tempest-tossed,
and
to their children

YOU COULD SAY THAT my father was a watchmaker by trade, but that would be like saying that Nijinsky liked to dance. Fixing watches was not only his livelihood but his life. This skill had saved him when he had been imprisoned at the death camp of Dachau, during the Second World War, and he continued to fix watches until the day he died. Simon Taitz was nothing less than a restorer of time. And I was his daughter, born to continue in his lifework—restoration and repair.

The minutes in my childhood home went by slowly and deliberately. They were accounted for by an endless series of clocks. Like the burghers of some old village, they sat around me as I listened to their secrets. Some kept the true hour; others were broken, chiming irregularly with dings and false, elaborate windups that led to weird silence. A few bombastically tolled the hours with notes that spread and reverberated. I was mesmerized by the whirly rotations within glass bell jars. I loved and feared the old cuckoos, with pendulums like overgrown Bavarian acorns. Clang and tick, pickaxe and wheel, a real hurly-burly.

My favorite was the one that sat on the breakfront in our apartment. Despite its size, this small mantel piece boomed throughout the house like an eight-foot grandfather clock. "Westminster chimes," my father proudly explained as he wound it, a beautiful British diapason of notes, sometimes long, sometimes short, and ending with a hearty, chest-full *boom-boom-boom.* My father's chest was large and round, his voice deep and resonant. I often thought that clock spoke for him and the dignified truth inside him. Time was company; it never left you. A look at a pleasant, numbered face, and you'd practically hear it say: "Yes, I'm here. See? I'm still marking the minutes. You can count on me."

When I think of my father's face, I see the loupe, the watchmaker's special magnifying glass. It was a small tube of black-painted metal worn on one eye, a mini-telescope that fit into the optical orbit as though it were part of the skull. Through the glass, my father surveyed a microcosmic ward of ailing tickers. His domain opened up with the tiny click of a pocket-watch door, releasing a magical world in which minute gears spun clockwise, counterclockwise, and back and forth, each with its own rhythm. Daily, he sat at his wooden workbench, presiding over the internal secrets of clocks, each revealing its tiny pulse as he restored it to the natural, universal order.

I thought of my father as a magical man and was in awe of him.

"See what's inside? Still alive," he'd say, opening the back of a pocket watch. My father could reverse time; my father could reverse fate. He could fix a broken face, a cracked and faded lens, and make it clear and true again. He could make a dead heart beat.

Though the phrase *Arbeit macht frei* was the notorious

banner welcoming doomed souls to slavery in Auschwitz, my father did, in fact, feel freed by his work. It relaxed him into a state of patient grace. By the time I was born, he had been fixing clocks and watches for nearly three decades. Simon had learned his trade back in Lithuania, apprenticing to a master as a boy of fourteen. His father had died when he was three, when Cossacks, rampaging through his village, shot the young miller, leaving behind a young widow and three helpless children. This story was my first narrative.

"Poor Bubbe Sonia!" I would say about my paternal grandmother, after whom I was named.

"'Poor' nothing," my father would answer. "She was a special woman, strong and brave."

This Sonia Taitz, the original one, buried her husband on their land, sold the millstones, and fled their riverside home, escaping into what my father called "deep Russia." I always imagined a dark, Slavic forest, and a young, Snow White–like woman, surrounded by menacing branches. Bright eyes in the night, sadists and murderers watching her and her three little children, my father, as in a fairy tale, the youngest. Her favorite.

The eldest, a bookish, lanky boy called Aaron, was sent away to wealthy relatives. They were not kind to him, and ultimately he ran away to Palestine and did manual labor with other raw immigrants. The middle child, Paula, was blue-eyed, dimpled, and flirtatious. After marrying hot and young, she and her husband were sent to Siberia by the Communists.

Simon was left alone to support his mother. A gifted athlete, he enjoyed the Lithuanian winters, skating around Kovno (as the Jews called Kaunas), racing through woods and villages, flying forward into his manhood. Though he would rather have studied and become a doctor, he considered himself lucky to find that he loved his trade, and by his early twenties was a master himself, with a workshop and trained apprentices of his own. When inducted into the Lithuanian army, he enlisted with enthusiasm and loved the physicality of it, the discipline. On his return, flush with confidence, he opened a watch store, then another; he bought himself a Harley Davidson, top of the line. But when the Communists invaded, he was forced to "nationalize" his business, as well as the Harley. Still, he survived, he thrived; he supported his widowed mother. In the evenings, he danced at parties.

When, however, the Nazis invaded Lithuania, Simon began planning ways of escape. Good Christian friends had offered him documents, and he had considered booking passage to Australia with his mother. She, however, was frightened of starting her life again so far away. So he stayed behind with her.

"That's why she died, right?" I was trying to figure out causes and avoidable, fixable mistakes. He had almost died as well; he was one of the very few Jews from his part of the world who had not.

"Who knows why she died?"

"No, Daddy, she had to keep moving. She got stuck!"

"I, too, my little Sonia. We all got stuck somewhere. But by a miracle, God heard my prayers, and I survived."

My father considered himself lucky to have become a watchmaker. Lawyers, businessmen, and even doctors went to the gas chambers, but his humble, practical skill was needed. This portable trade saved his life. Simon had been assigned to fix the time for the Nazis, who prized punctuality. As he explained to me, Germans respected his ability, eventually giving him his own workshop within the camp. A part of him reveled in this odd esteem, even (or especially) coming from his enemies and captors.

"The Germans admired a well-functioning machine. They loved order and discipline and I gave them that. Their watches and clocks came in broken and came out 'ticktock' perfect. So in some way we understood one another."

The watchmaker's trade was all that my father carried with him when he came to America in 1949, but again it was enough. After a few years of working in-house at Omega, the prestigious watch company, he began renting a little shop on the West Side of Manhattan, on Broadway and Sixty-third Street. Eventually, Lincoln Center would be built next door to this modest location, and he would befriend (and fix the watches of) great artists and impresarios; for now, he sat in his little jewelry shop in the middle of a tough neighborhood.

Hooting groups of teenagers ran by the store, hitting the windows with baseball bats. On a few occasions they smashed in the glass, shattering his storefront and grabbing watches by the trayful. My father chased them down the street, tackling the stragglers, grabbing back his treasures from their loosening fists. Carefully, he laid them back in their usual places in the trays, unafraid of anything but more degradation, more loss. He would truly rather die, now, than be bested by bullies and criminals. And he was not about to die. He installed heavy iron gates that at the beginning and the end of his long workday he slid over the windows with a long, loud set of clangs and a final bang. Then he installed a sensitive alarm system, so sensitive that any rattle of the gates would lead to an emergency call to the police, and another to our home. There was always a sense of potential disaster in that little West Side store, and the gates themselves, fastened by an enormous lock, seemed more a shock than a comfort to me.

Interspersed with the drama of thugs and thieves came the peacefulness of my father's labor. Simon was, I suppose, used to functioning around crises, always able to restore himself to calm productivity as maelstroms faded. A laminated wooden OMEGA, written in large gold letters, hung over his head as he sat quietly at his workbench, attesting to his ranking as a master. Omega was my father's Yale and his Harvard. Around him lay a little store lined with glass showcases and mirrors that my mother endlessly polished. Within the showcase lay velveteen trays holding jewelry; my mother wiped these treasures daily with a chamois cloth to make them sparkle.

And work soothed his soul as nothing else could. With the loupe in his eye, my father seemed to see everything. Even when a customer came into the store, he might not look up, so immersed was he in the intricate mysteries of his timepieces. My mother, his assistant in the shop, would dash up to them and eagerly say, "Can I help you?" Sometimes they were there to look at a ring, or try bracelets on their arms, and she would get busy and pull out some velveteen trays. Most often, however, they had heard of my father, and wanted a bit of his time.

"I'm waiting for the watchmaker," they would say.

A glass separated him from his customers, the way a curtain might separate the holy from the Holy of Holies. Only when it was time, only when an issue was settled in his mind, would my father lay down his work, pop out his loupe, and look up. Then he would say, with utter seriousness, each word seeming to take on its fullest meaning:

"How may I be of service to you?"

From deep within pockets, purses, bags, and briefcases would emerge a beloved old wristwatch, an antique pocket watch, or a large, priceless antique clock. Unwrapping, exposing, handing treasures over to my father's side of the glass, they would part with their heirlooms. He would look at the timepiece, first without the loupe, and then with it—opening the back with tiny tools as the customer stood back, scarcely breathing. Sometimes he would admire the secret paintings within secret doors (pastorals, portraits) or a clever repeater, a special toll, or ticking capability.

"Yes, I think I can make this repair," he would finally say. "When you come back, your treasure will be beating."

Naming Ceremony

I TOOK MY FIRST BREATH less than a decade after the flames of the Holocaust had ended. Embers glittered in the ashes, and the last plumes of smoke still hung in the air. Notwithstanding the busy, ticking timepieces, the atmosphere at home was thick with the past. I cannot remember being born into my own world, my own time frame. I was born into my parents' world, the world of refugees, immigrants, survivors.

It was dark in my apartment in Washington Heights, a leafy uptown enclave of immigrants perched on the Hudson. We lived in tenements with fire escapes, railroad flats where only the front rooms caught a breeze. Still, we were happy to come inside, climb the staircases, lock the heavy front doors to our apartments, and be safe and unbothered.

When we peeped out the front windows, the world outside was lively with screaming children playing stickball, hopscotching, or simply bouncing their balls against the sooty courtyard walls. Segregated by mere streets, we lived among hearty Irish handymen, ponytailed Puerto Rican girls who attended the Mother Cabrini convent school up the block, and the contained, devout German Jews who had lived in the neighborhood for decades. My parents were part of the most recent arrivals—Yiddish-speaking Polish and Lithuanian Jews who'd been spat out of Europe by a blast from Hades.

The fact that my older brother and I were alive, new Jews born after Hitler had promised to annihilate all the undesirables on the planet, was to my parents a sign and a miracle. My father and mother were both concentration camp survivors. Not victims—survivors, people who had looked death in the face and rebutted it. They had been slaves, with razor-nicked heads and skeletal bodies; they had scrounged for rotten potato peels and woken up alongside corpses; they had pleaded for their lives and run from guns and gasses, pits and ovens. They had prayed and promised and sensed, in my father's case particularly, the answering voice of God. Their belief, they felt, had saved them, and so, unlike many others, they kept on believing. I never thought of them as weak, but as God-like warriors themselves, however wounded.

At the time of my birth, an unruffled state of mind was, theoretically, available to most Americans. There was a world of conspiratorially bland, amusing entertainment, a corny embrace of normalcy. Still, the healing banality, the soothing crackle of black-and-white television, gray flannel suits, and blank-faced furniture was not peace to my folks, but hypocrisy. They felt a certain contempt for those vapid, idle Americans who didn't appreciate the true magnitude, the nightmarish depth, of existence, who persisted in focusing on what my parents called *narishkeit* (foolishness)—with their golf and their martinis, their beehive or Brylcreem hairdos and hulking two-car garages.

Me, at first I loved *narishkeit*. Until I started school, my best friend was the television. I ruthlessly daydreamed about a "Dad" who smoked a pipe while sitting in a lounger, offering bemused yet well-considered advice. I wanted a slim-hipped "Mom" who wore heels in the house, a ruffle-edged apron tied about her trim waistline. My father sported thin, white, sleeveless undershirts, with fringed prayer garments above, the latter in observance of the biblical law to wear just such a garment. The outfit was completed by the bottom half of a suit, neatly creased and belted. He had no concept of leisure except for the Sabbath day, on which he prayed and tried to rest. Hence, no baseball caps, no sneakers, no tennis sweaters—it was either the whole suit, with a tie, and tie pin—or this undershirt-based ensemble.

With the upper body of a circus strongman and a bald head, my father looked like Yul Brynner as the despot of Siam in *The King and I.* He had a similar dangerous accent and charismatic aura. His posture was military; his carriage, aristocratic. Even his vocal timbre was the same, Slavic and deep. When I called him "Dad," he'd mimic darkly.

"Dad? *Dad?*"

In his voice, it sounded like "Ded? *Ded?*"

He would roar, "You want me to be DEAD?" He seemed ready to deal with that threat, as he had too many times before.

So "Daddy" would do just fine.

My mother, estrogen to his androgen, wore busily floral "housedresses," which closed with snaps, or one long zipper from neck to knees. In the kitchen, she and her mother, who had also survived, stirred pots together. On her small feet she wore pink calfskin slippers called *shlurkes*. While my grandmother sat, emitting a sense of sepulchral gloom, her daughter scurried around, mopping, dusting, spraying polish on the heavy mahogany furniture, shining away with assorted rags. As she cleaned, she wore a permanent, almost ecstatic sheen of perspiration and would sometimes stand by an open window and let breezes blow on her face, eyes closed as gauzy white curtains danced in the air.

"Oy, a mechayeh!" she would say. Oh, this makes me live.

In our home, the language was Yiddish. I did not then know that this German/Hebrew blend I spoke, my first language and mother tongue, was dying, spoken as it was primarily by survivors of the Holocaust in Europe. It was only when the dark wooden doors of our television set were opened like an ark, the set clicked on to slowly reveal another world, that I realized our family spoke one language, but the rest of America spoke another. English was cleaner and clackier; it was more sensible and far less tender. People who spoke English were lucky and immune. They really knew what they were doing.

Every morning, I ran into the living room and swung open the TV doors to search for paradise. I turned on the set to watch a show called *Romper Room*, then waited as the TV's inner light began to glow, expanding. There she was: a calm, smiling lady, holding up a magic glass to her face. The goddess of children. Through it, she could see every kid in America. The lady would say:

"I see Bobby and Nancy and Anne-Marie. I see Richie and Stevie and Mary-Lou. I see Jeffrey and Billy and Susie and Chris. I see . . ."

"YOU SEE *ME*! I'M RIGHT *HERE*!"

I stood before her, jumping up and down on our frayed green carpet. This was how I watched television: standing on my spot, swaying, praying, desperate to contact the world outside my world. (The area where I stood was growing thread bare; I could see the beginnings of a dun mesh below the crushed nap.) I hopped on one foot for Captain Kangaroo. I showed my frilly panties to suave Sandy Becker. I twirled in tribute to the flickering cathode ray image of Ricky Ricardo, Lucy's Latino, an accented immigrant like my parents.

I was besotted by the fact that Lucille Ball and Desi Arnaz had married each other, so in love that their show began and ended with a gleaming satin pillow on which was scripted their blended name—"Desilu." They had crossed a great divide and met in the middle, like a fairy-tale kiss that broke all curses born of cultural distance.

"I see Kevin and Linda . . ."

"Call my name, lady! Call 'Sonia'!"

For that, of course, was my name. In Yiddish it was Shayna.

Sonia, much less Shayna, wasn't on the list of possibilities, unless the magic mirror lady could take a U-turn into a vat of savory schmaltz and say, with a thick, Semitic catch in her throat:

"Oy! Wait a minute! Now I see Ruchel and Dvora and Selma and Yizkhak and Menny'shu. Gevalt! I see Maxie, Irving, Irwin, Perel'le and Yacccchhhhim!!!"

Romper Room lady couldn't take that U-turn. It was I who had to.

"Hey, I know what you can call me in American!" I exclaimed to my parents with can-do optimism, as though I were teaching them to do the peppermint twist (which I myself was then learning from a show called *American Bandstand*). Often, they asked me how to say something in English, which they never completely mastered.

They were especially shocked by colloquialisms like "Get out of here!"

"This is polite to say?" my father would ask wonderingly. (He was also puzzled by the violent expression "son of a gun.")

"Sure, you say it when you don't believe someone. Like, someone tells you that they are gonna be on a TV show. And you can't believe it, so you say, 'No! Get out of here!'"

"Get out of here," said my father.

"Get out of there," said my mother.

My grandmother was silent. Finally, she muttered, in Yiddish:

"We already got out. What they want from us??"

"So what do you tell us about your name, now, Sonialeh?" asked my mother, lightly dipping a Swee-Touch-Nee teabag into a handled glass of boiling water. We were sitting down to breakfast in the kitchen. Pigeons flapped on the window-sill, and on our round, oilcloth-covered table sat butter, sour cream, rye and black breads, hunks of farmer cheese, and cut-glass dishes of preserves.

"You can call me 'Susie' now!" I blared. The sound of my high, ridiculous voice hung in the air.

"Huh, that's dumb," said my brother, who often sensed that his little sister was off.

My father stared at me for a moment, biding his time. He spread a thin layer of blueberry jam on his toast. It rasped like the weekend bristles on his chin, which, when in a good mood, he let me scratch with my fingertips. And then, he intoned, in his basso profundo, with dignity, slowly:

"Sonia, be proud of your name. My mother, she should rest in peace, who you are named for, died by the hands of those Nazis, murderers, may their names be erased from the world."

The Susies and Nancies were not named for the victims

of psychopaths whom one was never allowed to forget. They skipped down the street, pigtails bouncing. They giggled, teased, and wrinkled their noses. Their parents found them adorable, "spoiled them rotten"; they braided their hair and put satin ribbons in it.

To my father's last comment my mother would not fail to respond.

"At least she lived her life, your mother. She grew up, she married, she had children. My poor little brothers died young, teenagers! Shot like animals! They had no life at all! What did they do to deserve it? Why did they have to die?"

Three years older, my brother tended to escape these inquisitions, and now, grabbing half a rye bread, cucumber, and butter sandwich, ran off to his room. Auburn-haired, freckle-faced, Manny was a whirlwind of activity with a pocketful of bottle caps and marbles. Sitting him down was a challenge, much less posing to him the Greatest Hits of Moral Philosophy. But me, I was a brooder. From the time I had begun asking "Why?" they had begun to respond, "Yes, why? What do you think?" And I had attempted to answer.

At night, after everyone fell asleep, I would get up, run to my brother's room next door, and grab the flashlight out of his bedside drawer. Back in bed, lemur eyes and flashlight to the page (so I would not wake my grandmother, with whom I shared a room), I'd open my picture book of Genesis, worrying myself. The sacrifice of Isaac was a special concern.

Why does Abraham try to hurt his own child? I'd creep out again, fretting to myself, running in the dark corridor past Manny's room, the bathroom, the kitchen, the living room, and then, at last, bursting though the French doors, into the sanctuary of my parents' bedroom.

"What do you mean, Sonia? He was obeying God," my

father might say, stirring, turning to face me. My father's side of the bed was the one near the window. In the night, it would be lit by the passing cars, and he would wake up to my voice with kind concern, eyes coming alive in the flickering light. Being called in the middle of the night to discuss the sacrifice of Isaac was an actual pleasure for the man. He'd pat my head affectionately.

"What a smart little girlie," he'd murmur. "With her good questions."

"Do you think it was easy for Abraham?" my mother would add, still lying down. "He suffered, too." She, too, could talk about suffering in her sleep.

"Yes, but—don't you think maybe Abraham should have talked with God a little? For his kid's sake?"

"You think talking to God is enough?" said my mother, raising her head to look at me. "If only . . ."

"Yes, it can be enough sometimes," my father demurred. He was sure his prayers had saved him in the war.

"Maybe someone could find the right exact sentences!" I'd persist. I didn't think my father's prayers had done that much good. He and my mother still seemed so upset. God had let bad people hurt them.

"Maybe you can find them, then, the words we are all looking for," my father added. "But now, go back to sleep so you have the strength to look for them."

And now, at the breakfast table, my mother was asking me her own stumper of the day. She turned to me and pleaded: "Why did my brothers have to die? Why? They were fine, good boys!"

My grandmother glared at me. As well as I knew the English language, and good as I was at school, I did not have the answers to all questions, theirs or mine.

My middle name, Judith, was in honor of these two brothers, my grandmother's lost children. I wished it were Jane.

"All right, fine, so this one you don't know, I don't know, no one knows," said my mother, sweeping up the table crumbs with one cuffed hand. "But remember them, *mein kind*," she added, her hand now full of collected scraps. After a minute, she stepped on the garbage can lid and tossed them away with a *tsk*.

In telling me their stories, my parents felt that they were nourishing my character as a Jewish daughter. The last thing either of them wanted me to be was flighty, or free of history. To them, telling me about the Holocaust was like telling me about the secrets of the cosmos. I just wasn't clear about what it all meant—that the universe, God included, was a big bully? I could never agree to that. Inwardly, I fought that. Their little soldier was a double agent, half in love with hope.

"OK, Mommy," I said, wriggling away from the folding wooden stepstool that served as my kitchen chair. "I'll remember your brothers."

But first I want to see another commercial for Patty Playpal.

"Do you want more to eat something, Sonialeh?"

"Zie hat gantz nit gegessen," muttered my grandmother. "Gornisht."

"I did eat! I want to go watch TV."

Life was not monstrous in that box, nor, I suspected, in the America it portrayed. In America, God was a big ray of sunshine on a neatly mown lawn. He was the smile on happy parents' faces, beaming joy on their children.

The living room was adjacent to the kitchen. I was about to turn on the TV again when I heard my father's raised voice.

"Wait, Gita. Did you say *shot*? Your brothers, they were shot? On my mother, they didn't want to waste a bullet. They shoved them all, naked, into the showers. And what sprays out? Not water, gas. Suffocated. A horrible death. It makes me sick to talk about it."

There was a moment of silence. And then my mother, rebounding:

"But at least she had a life!"

That was part of the competition—my life was worse than yours. It was part of the great theme. The Jews suffered more. You don't know from suffering. You didn't have a potato peel? I didn't have teeth. You didn't have teeth? You were lucky—from me, they pulled out all my teeth, one by one . . .

"All right, Gita, my mother Sonia, she should rest in peace, had a life, once. And I am glad of it."

I wanted a life, too, I thought, turning on the television that made happy faces come glowingly to life. And there she was, the Romper Room lady. The show was not over, and soon she would take up her mirror.

One day, I knew, she would see me. My mother would see me; my father would take out his loupe and really see me. The Sonia who was not *her* dead brothers or *his* dead mother, but a real live girl.

Arpeggios and Arpège

My mother, Gita, was seven years younger than Simon in age, and lighter, more pastel in temperament. Most people, including myself, found her fragrant, pretty, cuddly, cute. She possessed a certain ineradicable joie de vivre that fate had not taken from her. She was stubborn in her happiness; she could hum through her frustrations, and a good apple or orange could change her day entirely.

"Oy," she would say, the *oy* in this case meaning something positive: "Oy, is this good!" And she would be talking about a bite of McIntosh apple (her favorite), or the simple act of coming home into a warm house in the winter, or a cool house in the summer. The windows open, no air conditioning (a little stuffy), and still she would say, "Oy, a mechayeh!"

Gita's childhood and early teen years had been brought to an abrupt halt by politics; from the time of the Nazis she had stayed hip-close to her mother. Thus, she remained something of a child, a good girl who causes no trouble and asks no questions. As a condition of marriage, her only request was that her mother, Liba, who had survived the concentration camps with her, be allowed to live with them. My father, in turn, requested that his wife be a helpmate, working in his store. (Liba would take care of the children.) Gita had agreed—and spent the rest of her life catering tirelessly to him until the day he died.

A piano virtuoso, her conservatory career had been ruined by the war. She had had to leave her piano behind to go to the ghetto (and later, the concentration camp); she had even lost her music books and practice notebooks. Gita was not used to mopping floors, cooking endless meals, or helping out in a watchmaker's store. Nor had she anticipated the suddenness and severity of her new husband's wild temper. Since becoming his wife, she had learned about a merciless demon deep inside him. It was a kind of cuckoo, I sometimes thought, something that popped out of the works and then popped back.

"GITA!!" he'd roar. "Are you really bad or just plain stupid?" If an argument occurred during a meal—which it often did, as meals forced closeness—he'd slam his plate, food and all, to the floor as she wept, as much over the wasted food as the shards of broken china.

This cuckoo-man had no pity for a child-bride who cried easily and who wanted nothing more than to be romanced, as in a dream that had been interrupted when the Nazis had stomped in. Debussy, Czerny, and especially Chopin, she said, had led her to great visions of love. Now, she raced about him urgently, like a child trying to please but fearing she wouldn't, rising early each morning to cook and pack her husband's lunch (fried flounder in a buttered roll, a tomato, an apple) and fill a tartan-patterned thermos full of coffee (Nescafé, instant). Simon would leave early, descending into the subway when it was still dark outside. In his late thirties, it was up to him to climb out of poverty once again, with no family but a twittering wife and her sullen, traumatized mother.

When Gita came to work, she would be sent on errands to find gears and springs and watch straps, or told to straighten the showcases and arrange the jewelry neatly. Regardless of how much polishing she did, the place always seemed to smell of dusty smother to me—a feeling of gray in the air, a rime of whiteness on the black velveteen trays. The steel light fixtures seemed dull, too, the fluorescent rods within them colorless and dead. Cold chrome was everywhere—on the lamps, on the edges of the glass, in the heavy-based mirrors that stood on every table so that customers could see themselves.

I loved smoothing the honey-colored wood panels in the back of the showcases. They seemed warmer and more alive. With the twist of a tiny key they opened, sliding apart as I'd help my mother reach a tray to bring up to the counter. My father's workbench, too, was of a worn, tawny wood. My parents were selling jewelry as well as watches, so Gita busied herself with wrapping boxes for paramours buying modest rings and bracelets (these young men made her smile), or dowagers buying large "cocktail rings" with semiprecious stones. Her equipment was a roll of silver paper, a monumental, weighted tape dispenser, and cherry-red velveteen bows, which she tied with meticulous care. My mother hummed as she worked; she was born happy; she had had almost eighteen happy years; and now she would always revert to joy by nature.

Yet there was a precarious quality to her happiness; when, unpredictably, its vague borders were touched, she would weep, or close down in disdainful rejection. She never told her mother how her husband's shouting and insults hurt her, but she did, very early, tell me, in her own special locution:

"He is trying to make from me a Nothing." Even the Nazis had not done that, she would bitterly observe. He was as strong and strict as any German, and proud of it.

He, in turn, would confide to me that he was baffled to have married such a silly woman. He found her "moods" ridiculous. His mother had never shown moods, not even when she had had to bury her husband and run with her three children into "deep Russia." My mother would respond, under her breath but in my earshot, that his mother sounded like she literally did wear army boots.

"Oy," she'd say, smiling mischievously, "I would run from such a sourpot!

"And that is why he's such a strict officer," she would conclude, dousing herself before bedtime with Arpège, her pastel nightgowns silky and cool to the touch. "And now he orders me."

The hierarchy was not always clear. She would stop at nothing to bait him, incessantly nagging, chattering, kissing his neck or hand, asking the same question over and over, like Tevye to his wife:

"Do you love me?"

And he would say, "Gita. You know that words are meaningless to me. 'I love you, I love you, I love you'—pah! So cheap and stupid!"

When he raised his voice and got annoyed, she'd smile a little. His raised voice told her she'd made contact. Impact.

"Sourpot," she'd whisper to me, and wink.

I was torn between their points of view. No matter how cruel the arguments, my mother seemed, on some level, to enjoy herself even as my father's face turned so red I was worried he'd die on the spot. It exhausted me, having to choose between his passionate, patriarchal sense of being wronged, and her easygoing, but slightly sadistic, resistance and feigned bafflement.

Yet every Sabbath, for all the arguments, they would sit at the head of a candlelit table like a royal couple. After lunch each Saturday, they would eventually take a long stroll together through the neighborhood, hand in hand in the late afternoon. They loved this walk, always ending it in the leafy groves of Fort Tryon Park, strolling by the flower beds. Other leisurely walkers tipped their hats and greeted them, standing in the dancing shade of plane trees to chat about their children or grandchildren.

It would take my parents nearly their entire lives to realize how well suited they were. Both were industrious, innocent, generous, and honest; both had seen the same world disappear. Both had left everything behind, and would never—could never—return. There was nothing to return to; their culture, what was left of it, was simply transported, bruised as it was, to America and Israel. On these strange New York City streets, stumbling with the language, scraping to reinvent themselves, they were each other's only harbor.

UNLIKE HER HUSBAND, my mother had not lost everything in the war; she had saved her own mother, whom she worshipped. In the ghetto, she had hidden Liba in the "eggbox," she told me, sitting on it as the guards tromped around looking for helpless old people to kill. Later, during "selection," the entire Jewish populace had had to line up and have Nazis decide which ones were to live and which to die. Her mother had been sent to the bad line (meaning incapable of labor, marked for immediate death), my mother, to the good. She had, however, in a panic, run from her line to join her mother.

"I wanted only to be with my Mamaleh," she said, sometimes with a meaningful, slightly resentful glance in my direction. Already, she could see (rightly) that I would not carry on the symbiosis of mother-daughter to the death. For a start, I was always restless by her side, especially in the kitchen. Not a good eater. Not interested in pots and pans and bubbling stews. My father's daughter, intense and always cogitating.

"So I ran like a crazy, not thinking; they could have shot me! And then, in a minute, I was with my mother. And then I did her work, and I kept her warm, and I begged her to keep trying to live. And together, thanks God, we survived."

Her mother, Liba, had welcomed death. She had watched her sons leaving the ghetto, ostensibly on a work detail, only to find out that they had been shot along with dozens of other hale young men. She had seen her husband sent away to be gassed in the Dachau concentration camp. Her daughter was all that was left to her, and this child would not abandon her—even if it meant her own death. They lived through the liberation together, and through the Displaced Persons camps, and they came together to America. Gita was just out of her teens when these events had begun to unfold.

Now, like her husband, she tried to master English. It would be their sixth language. They already knew Yiddish, Hebrew, Lithuanian, Russian, and—due to four postwar years in Deutschland—German. Before the war, her family had had cooks and laundresses and cleaning ladies. Now, Gita did her best, learning to cook and clean the apartment—both in a generous, copious, and imperfect fashion. She learned to hurtle downtown on the subway to run a business with her driven, ultra-serious husband.

Although he frightened her, she respected him. "At least he is not a runner, a liar, a drinker, a gambler—he is a good, honest, Jewish man." She sometimes added, "and he has a beautiful soul—like a poet." His violent outbursts of rage only confirmed this image. There was something prophetic and passionate in him—something almost inexpressible. Like most people, she found him fascinating, charismatic. He had a real aura, haunting and deep.

Once, when I was about eleven and accompanying my parents on the subway to Radio City Music Hall, my mother, happy to be on a jaunt, wiggled her feet near the edge of the subway platform. It was warm outside. I remember that she wore a flowery summer dress with delicate shoes, like ballet slippers. In the center of these shoes, on top of her toes, was a little straw bouquet of fruit, complete with two small, shiny wooden cherries. I was staring at the pretty cherries as one of my mother's shoes fell off and landed in the tracks. These tracks were deep, dark, and dangerous.

Not hesitating, my father leaped down into the darkness. In a second, he held the shoe in his hand. I can still see him look up at us, smiling; I can see the cherries, shining like new hope. From far away, I began to hear the rumble of an oncoming train. My father, trying to climb back onto the platform, struggled through a few efforts, then, with a powerful leap, at last joined us. As I caught my breath, he placed the shoe on my mother's small foot. No question, her husband was a hero, a leader, someone to reckon with. You could be safe with him.

Each day together, she ran "like a crazy" to make his life easier—running to the store to work, home to cook, to the hospital when he was dying. From the day he met her, he was never alone; she was his constant helpmate.

In his heart of hearts, my father did love her. She had a beauty and lovability that he saw immediately, and he continued to see it until his dying day. This held their lives together, and bound her to him.

Eine Kleine Schwarzkopf

MY BIG BROTHER and I were left at home in the care of my elderly grandmother Liba. This figure, so beloved to my own mother, so precious that she would risk her own life to save her, was a puzzle to me. "Bubbe" was proud by nature, and scarcely resembled the woman in a picture that sat on the wall in my parents' bedroom. There, she was elegant, her hands inside a luxurious, dark fur muff, surrounded by three lovely children (my mother in long braids, her younger brothers in shining buttoned shoes) and a distinguished husband with a gentleman's neatly groomed moustache. Liba had had cooks and maids; she had loved singing; she had gloriously driven her own horse and carriage around town—all this I was told by my mother, who idolized her. But the Bubbe I met was exhausted, extinguished, and favored sitting in the darkest corner, by a window where pigeons flapped dustily in the airshaft. Knees apart under a heavy dark dress, she emitted an aura of bitter knowledge, which she did not wish to share. She spoke to me in brief, short bursts of Yiddish: "Zetz." "Ess." "Herr opp." "Schweig." (Sit. Eat. Stop it. Be quiet.)

Thick-haired, long-limbed, busy, and mischievous, Manny loved to tease me. I was pleased that he paid any attention to me at all; I existed mostly in a dense fog of boredom. Sometimes he'd pick up a mirror and, catching the sunlight in it, tell me to "chase the spot." I amused myself by obeying him, darting like a kitten after circles of light on the wall. He'd display my hilarious stupidity to his friends, and I'd willingly repeat the kitten-chase. It pleased me to humor him. Sometimes, as a special treat, he'd take me up and down the black-painted stairs of our small apartment building, looking for "treasure" in the garbage cans. I fully believed in his abilities as loot-finder when we found a fully intact roulette wheel, impressive in its weight and heft. It gave my brother pleasure to see me spin and spin it, not caring that the chips were gone, not to mention the all-important ball that determined one's luck.

He nicknamed me "José"—a reference to my blue-black hair, a rarity among European Jews. It was meant as an obliterating (if witty) put-down, and it made my brother giggle until tears fell from his eyes: the Puerto Ricans who lived on the other side of Upper Broadway were even poorer than we—and he had dubbed me a Puerto Rican *boy*. I couldn't even imagine myself to be one of the girls who attended Mother Cabrini, the convent school across the street from my house that seemed a holy bastion of white knee socks, plaid skirts, and general dark sexiness. My own dampened appeal was my mother's doing; she chopped my hair herself, uneven bangs and all, and kept it short for convenience. I looked not so much like a José but like a good Chinese child (of indistinct gender), glum in the rice fields.

My brother's presence, even his teasing, represented a life force to me, and I looked up to him. When he started school, I took comfort in the blessed television set, missing and envying others his company. I believe my brother was sent to school a year early because he was active and rambunctious. With him away for several hours a day, my grandmother could settle into a less eventful life with just one child. It was thought that as a girl I would be easier to take care of.

Neither my mother nor grandmother fully trusted my coal-tar mop of hair, which hinted, at the same time, of wildness and vulnerability. It came from my father's side of the family, the poorer side, the side that apprenticed fatherless boys to be watchmakers, and was therefore déclassé. It was, furthermore, dangerous to look as . . . as "exotic" as I did. There was a word for me (did the Nazis invent this?)—I was a Schwarzkopf—a black-head. From the beginning, my mother and Bubbe hinted that my inky hair was excessive. It was too intense, like a tambourine-shaking gypsy running barefoot down the street. (They didn't actually use those exact words— but they did call me a "tzigane.") The little girls they openly admired had infantile, softly curled blonde hair—ironically, the Christian ideal of a cherub. "Oh, how beautiful," they'd say, looking at a child with flaxen ringlets. "Oy, vi shein."

It did not help that hair-color commercials kept blaring on the television:

IS IT TRUE BLONDES HAVE MORE FUN???

WHY NOT BE A BLONDE AND SEE?

And, more hauntingly:

IF I'VE ONLY ONE LIFE, LET ME LIVE IT AS A BLONDE!!!

These insistent pieces of advice made me anxious—what was I to do about this problem? For a few years, I would take the flax out of our boxes of *etrogs*—lemony citrons, imported from Israel, which we bought each year at Sukkot, the autumn harvest holiday. I'd wear this beige-yellow packing material on my head.

"Do I look like a beautiful blondie now?" I'd ask hopefully.

"Not exactly," my mother would answer, laughing and plopping some flax on her head as well.

On the television set, blonde girls seemed to be the true darlings. They played with their toys and dolls in a perfect world of loveliness. Their mothers knew how to be pretty, too, and used Clairol, after which they would run across fields in such a lovely way, to a beautiful embrace. Whenever I mentioned these important American, transformative purchases to my parents—this wondrous doll, that versatile Silly Putty, a bottle of dye—they would ignore me. Both had to work all day, with little to show for it. Our carpet was increasingly threadbare, the sofa lumpy and worn (my mother had taken to throwing fringed covers on it). They had other things to think about. I however, tended to focus on one thing at a time, about which I would fixate with great dedication and readiness to act.

IS IT TRUE BLONDES HAVE MORE FUN?

If it was, where did that leave me? The un-fun black-haired child who faced me in the mirror, I had been told, would have immediately been spotted as a *Jude* and killed by the Nazis. "A blonde you could sometimes hide," went the brutally honest kitchen-table wisdom in my home. (So, I thought, blondes *did* have more fun—they could live to see another day!) They'd be peeling potatoes together, my mother and grandmother, comfortable with their expertise in the race-logic of maniacs.

"But you could not save *such* a black-hair."

"Nothing could be done."

"And the big, dark eyes."

"Gornisht vilt ihr helfen." Nothing will help her.

Potatoes boiling in bubbling water; peels tossed into the garbage can with a guillotine's thunk of the lid. The matriarchs had spoken.

I'd run from their words. All the rooms in the apartment followed a narrow corridor. All but one faced a dark and sooty alleyway, gray-pocked as a moonscape. I'd gravitate to any source of optical novelty, staring with fascination at the linoleum flooring in my and Manny's bedrooms: pixilated and sparkly, pink with *tromp l'oeil* ice cubes in mine, beige with sparkling red, blue, and green pick-up sticks in his. All the walls were mute with beige, even in the children's rooms—no paintings, no drawings, not even a calendar. There was an Indian headdress in my brother's room, with long, multicolored feathers, and a cap gun that smelled marvelous when shot, which he treasured; he also had a splendid velvet bag full of marbles. These were, to me, the gardens of Giverny and the Taj Mahal, and I stared into these orbs and the twirly helix-suspensions inside them as often as I could. I looked for stars, fairies, and sparkles everywhere.

My parents' front windows faced the street, bringing in the sky, ringing sounds of children's laughter, and the comforting adult burble of people who sat in lawn chairs, below, in the warm weather. Here is where my mother would stand, window open, to remind herself that she was young and alive and not a "Nothing." Those wonderful front windows let light—sunshine—into my parents' bedroom, illuminating their large wooden bed. Here, the sun caught motes of dust in a beam—a floating epiphany of shining, sunlit matter, which seemed to carry messages of hope. My brother told me they were "atoms" and I embraced his vision. I asked him if the pavements near our house, which had something shiny embedded in them, contained diamonds. He told me: "Of course they do!" These diamonds and magical atoms enlivened hundreds of my earliest hours.

IN THE SUMMERS, I would hear the celestial music of the Mr. Softee truck, which played its tune right outside my parents' window. *Outside*—what a glorious, windswept concept. I wanted to go down there; I wanted ice cream from the ice cream man; I wanted to follow that truck as one follows the circus. I wanted to dance, peel off my clothes, run!

Just above us lived a little girl about my age, Esther Plaut. Her parents, like most people in our building, were also Holocaust survivors. Mrs. Plaut, who worked from her home, was a stately seamstress with strong, wide hips and a gray-black bun like a bagel at the top of her head. Unlike my parents, she had a blue tattoo on her forearm, with a long sequence of numbers on it. The Plaut's front bedroom had been turned into a workroom where clients visited. In it stood several tailor's dummies—faceless torsos on which she pinned her dresses. Mrs. Plaut had a tremor, which I thought at the time was brought on by her Singer sewing machine, the pulsing engine of her workroom. Even when it was off, though, her arms would rattle, the numbers shaking and blurring into a light blue line like a touch of horizon.

Esther's mother was stoical but kind. Though they were poor, her parents indulged her with great toys: not only Barbies but Kens and Skippers and clothing and accessories and See 'n Says (clocklike toys with pull-strings that made barn sounds) and sixty-four crayons and white boards and blackboards and Parcheesi and Shari Lewis singing about Lamb Chop on a long-playing record. Every day, Mrs. Plaut stopped work to make us tuna with onions and celery and chocolate milk made with three pumps of U-bet syrup, and we sat in the kitchen and ate and drank (she even gave us straws), and it was heavenly. While we ate, she would lie on the couch and watch her soap opera. From the kitchen I could hear dramatic cries ("But I love you!") and the intermittent warning of organ music. We'd be quiet and listen. Later, our Barbies and Kens would kiss passionately, their plastic heads mashing and circling as we held their rigid bodies in the air.

Sometimes, Esther and I would go to the playground across the street and play hopscotch and potsy—a game that featured a metal apple-juice lid (donated by Esther's mother), which we threw with concentration onto the correct bit of chalked concrete. In the distance, I might see my brother with his friends playing Nok Hockey with cool authority. Manny would wink at me, and I'd feel proud to have not only a brother, but an older brother, someone who knew his way around a Nok-Hockey board, the pool table of the underage set.

In the evening, Esther's unassuming father, a slim, long-faced man who looked like Stan Laurel, would come home from work and run into Esther's arms, sweeping her up. Then, perhaps, we'd hear the Mr. Softee truck play its tinkling tune below. Mr. Plaut would run downstairs and get us each a cone, vanilla custard swirling in peaks, coated with chocolate sprinkles. He was a real "Poppa" sort of father—a softy himself, good and kind.

Esther and I would watch him through her front-facing window as he bought our ice creams. In front of the house, which featured a recessed and narrow courtyard, many of our other neighbors sat on light folding chairs, enjoying the breezy end of a hot day. The Yiddish that floated up to our window was soothing and familiar.

Upstairs, there was also a woman whose name I remember as Mrs. Schroodel, to whom, weekly, my mother would deliver vats of dill-scented chicken soup, afloat with carrots and thick with egg noodles (lockshen). She was an invalid, and I remember her apartment was full of breezes, floral cotton curtains dancing slowly by open windows. Mrs. Schroodel sat still in the center, weighty in her wheelchair. I remember that she seemed genuinely to like children, for she would exclaim, on seeing me in the doorway:

"Oy, ah zeeseh kind!" Oh, a sweet child!

She had a crystal dish of wrapped hard candies on her coffee table and urged me to take as many as I wanted. Some were amazing—hard on the outside, jelly on the inside. A surprise—love and even deeper love. The old lady watched me as I took the candies, smiling into my eyes. That dish was magical; there was never a time that it was not full of sweets, arranged on a circle of crystal that stood high up on a cobalt blue pedestal.

I played the part for her, the grateful tyke who takes a treat, making myself more lovable to fit snugly into Mrs. Schroodel's pure heart. In her eyes, I was a precious child, adored in herself, someone's "baby" and "kitten." I had it in me to climb up and sit on Mrs. Schroodel's lap, to cuddle there, and keep her company, like a faithful pet. As it was I sucked her candies and saved the wrappers, with their pretty pictures of cherries and peaches.

There was another shtetl to which many survivors moved when they could. This was a place called Riverdale, in the Bronx, an enclave far more suburban than my little enclave in Washington Heights. This was a huge step up. Before my brother and I were born, my parents and most of their friends had lived in tenements on the Lower East Side. My mother often remembered how her cousin, also named Gita, would carry her children up the narrow stairs to her fourth-floor walk-up.

"One on each hip, she would schlep."

She brought this up regularly, not merely to reminisce, but because this Gita, like most of my mother's circle, had begun to change gradually, rejecting my mother and her old-fashioned ways. As they became more and more successful at their makeshift trades (one collected "junk"; another, "scrap metal"), they grew more and more prosperous. These "modern" friends no longer talked about the Holocaust. They smoked Parliaments with recessed filters. They dyed their hair "ash" or "champagne" blonde. They bought Cadillacs and Lincoln Continentals and shopped at Saks Fifth Avenue (which, due to their accents, they amusingly pronounced "Seks"). They played bridge and gin rummy. They boasted of eating "Shrimp Cocktail" and "Clams Casino," wondering why on earth my parents didn't.

"Why don't you eat this? It's so good!"

"Why *do* you eat this—your grandpa was a rabbi!" my mother, who knew, would reply tartly.

We often traveled to Riverdale to celebrate one of the children's birthdays. Those children were so lucky, even if they were happy and thus (by my father's logic) so ignorant. I found it hard to think of our family as their superiors. Someone would have to pick us up in their car. We would sit like "sardines," as my mother lightheartedly described it (I'd be on someone's lap), as we left the city and headed out. Once there, we would crunch across a graveled, circular driveway and see the split-level where my mother's friend and former bridesmaid, another Sonia, lived with her successful husband, a manufacturer of hot-dog casings. Their house was one of the first beautiful things I had ever seen in real life. And Jews lived there—even Holocaust survivors. My heart would burst with longing for the tableau that opened before us as we spilled out of the backseat.

Sprinklers whispered on the lawn and from among them Sonia's daughter would emerge. Marlene was a beautiful tall girl, about my age, with long, wavy hair like Ava Gardner, and a rare, dimpled sweetness. She had a dog, a German shepherd called Thunder, who was kept in the garage (they had a garage!). As the parents drank cocktails, lounging on cushioned chaises in the backyard, the children were taken by a maid down to a carpeted, wood-paneled basement decorated with pink and white balloons. Our little cone hats were pink, too, with silver tassels, which seemed impossibly glamorous to me.

This was where heaven was on the map, but we had to leave after only a few hours. On our crushed drive back, the shameful ride of schnorrers, as I saw it, of poor beggars without the sense to have a Lincoln Continental, a split-level, or *even a dog*, I would grow dark and sulky. Marlene's father worked with *wieners*, and yet he'd figured out how to live here in America! What was wrong with my parents?

My parents were the only ones of their gang to continue to actually worship God as they had before the war. They stayed observant, insular and simple. My father kept working hard in his store, wearing his wash-and-wear, short-sleeved shirts, eating his lunch out of a brown paper bag (often reused; my mother may have been one of the world's first recyclers). My mother continued to wear housedresses and aprons. As her friends moved on to credit cards at Bonwit's and Bendel's, she kept shopping at Alexander's and John's Bargain Store, pulling endless wads of bills out of her capacious beige brassieres.

I wanted nothing more than to move to Riverdale and be rich, untroubled, secular, and superficial (my vision of the perfect American life), but my mean parents would have none of it.

"What you have is better than a big house or a stupid piece of *traif* (unkosher food) that gives them so much pleasure," my father would say privately. "These people, they've lost their sense of honor, abandoning traditions that have been kept for thousands of years all over the world." What he meant by "what we have" was something about values.

This was just like when I'd ask him if I was beautiful, and he'd say:

"What you have is more important than looks."

I knew what *that* meant.

"Oy, I could vomit," my mother would interject, "even thinking of eating such a crawling shrimp that is such a treat for them!"

"You have something far more precious: knowledge and tradition, and all the talents God gave you," my father would continue in his theme of "higher things."

I saw the point, but what I really wanted was a room with a canopy bed, a big dog, and a swing set.

"Can't I just have the dog?" I'd ask my mother, as she cut my hair into its standard pageboy.

"Of course! Your grandma and I are looking now for houses. Daddy says he wants a two-family, so we can have income. As soon as we find the right house, you can have a dog."

BESIDES THE BIBLE, there were few books in my house, short of the *Golden Book Encyclopedia*, a paperback dictionary, and later, a fascinating, importantly bound series of *Reader's Digest Condensed Books*. To allay my boredom, I was given dimes and allowed to run outside to the corner store and buy small "Golden Books" (from which I would scissor out pictures of dogs, sticking them into my treasure bag).

Then I discovered comic books. I enjoyed *Casper the Friendly Ghost*, who lived as a disembodied spirit, and his similarly afflicted friend, Wendy. Their plight was poignant, and familiar to me—they just wanted to make friends, and yet because they were different (having experienced death), everybody shunned them, like racist anti-Semites. The bigoted people's fear, of course, was misguided—Casper and Wendy could have been great assets to the community, had they only been included. They might have made a huge contribution to science, like Jonas Salk, inventor of the polio vaccine.

At the age of nine, I began to favor *Archie* comics, due

to the fascinating dating chronicles within. By sheer coincidence, these took place in *Riverdale*, where, besides the backyards and garages I already knew and envied, there was never anything to do but go on dates. I assumed this was what my parents' friends' lucky children would do, in time. All I could do was read, envy, and analyze. The rules of love and sex became as vital to me—and as open to analysis—as those of the Torah.

Betty and Veronica, who vied endlessly for Archie's love, had identical faces as drawn. Both had big eyes and great, fringed black lashes. Each had an upturned nose, and a glossy, full mouth. Each had a curvy, figure-eight body. The only real difference was that one had blonde hair; the other, black—and with that came the primal characteristics. Betty was nice and sweet and normal. Veronica was rich and cruel and sexy. The Hair Wars, begun by my mother's random comment about blondes, fanned by the Clairol company (and, before it, the Third Reich), could continue apace.

Studying old movies, I'd see that brunettes were the vamps, the bad girls, the femme fatales. I kept my eye on Sophia Loren, Natalie Wood, and an exciting pitch-black she-devil Schwarzkopf named Elizabeth Taylor. I began to see the world as bouncy Betties and vampy Veronicas. Who would rule Riverdale—perhaps the entire world? Blackies or blondies?

My mother, for her part, was a committed fan of certifiably "light" Doris Day (originally called Doris Mary Ann Von Kappelhoff, of German ancestry). She worshipped this blonde on Sundays. From an early age, my mother had taken my brother and me to the movies on weekends. Sometimes we stood on the world's longest line for the certified blockbusters at the Radio City Music Hall, but more often, she would whisk us around the corner to the RKO Coliseum for the latest Doris Day adventure. For two hours, my mother would experience vicarious bliss. On celluloid, Von Kappelhoff's life seemed clean, bright, and untroubled. Her platinum hair and flat blue eyes rendered her as impermeable as a new Formica countertop, not to mention her matching ensembles in the colors of sherbet, including many cute hats and matching handbags.

Though I would probably rather have seen *Bambi* or *The Absent-Minded Professor*, these neat parables seeped deeply into my budding female subconscious. James Garner, hmm? He really did seem to complete the picture, a playful, ha-ha-hearty hunk of human gonadotropin, putting the lady straight. The themes were brutal, reductive, sexy: a woman, however brisk, efficient, and head-tossing, needs something she doesn't even want to know she needs. She needs some caveman to grab her hair, screw up her movements, and set the robotics deliciously a-jangle. I got that, in some primordial way. When, at the ending of most of Doris's films, the man would carry her off kicking, I would feel strangely thrilled. The titles, too, begged for innuendo: *The Thrill of It All, That Touch of Mink.*

After the movies, my mother would wait until just a bit after the lights came on, and then, snapping into the present, would take us out to the kosher delicatessen. We'd eat crispy grilled hot dogs with sauerkraut, and thick, salty potato knishes, washed down with Dr. Brown's Black Cherry soda. It was blissful until the moment when we all thought, "Why did I eat that?" And then, the blessed belching:

"A grepsele aroys, a gezunt aroyn."

A little burp goes out, and health comes in.

Later, I'd mull over the charms of Doris Day (who I am

sure never *grepsed*), wondering why my mother loved her so much. She seemed ordinary to me, like a dental assistant. It was really the contrast between her predictable primness and the clog-clearing male energy that made these movies buzz. That, and her many ways of being indignant. "Hoo!" she'd say, about these menfolk, blowing a stray lock of hair out of her eyes. "The nerve!" She liked the drama of it, I concluded; I did, too.

Soon, I began to study my mother's movie magazines, periodicals with names like *Modern Screen* and *Hollywood Confidential.* I was possessed by these confidences, these insights into the mind. It was a way out of the gloomy gray and into the realms of Technicolor—an alternate reality. Through the stars my mother and I saw on the screen, to the learned commentaries we read in those deeply earnest periodicals, we shared a female world of passionate wonder.

The movie magazines were different from the ubiquitous gossip rags of today, with fewer pictures and far more story. Reverential in tone, the articles were accompanied by studio publicity shots, lit up in a way that evoked a poignant quest for the holy and the healing. Each page was packed with detailed, almost obsessive, analyses of the motives, needs, and hungers of its celestial characters, unironically known as the "stars." There were pages and pages of textual explanations for every kind of passionate aberration, usually delivered in the first person: "Why I need to be with Rex." "My painful childhood secret." Painful childhood secret? I flipped pages rapidly, learning to speed-read.

These stars had extraordinary needs and passions; often they had been wounded in their early years, and now could not get enough love (or anything else) to heal them. Judy Garland had once been given the terrible name Frances

Gumm, and her mother had been cruel to her in other ways as well. Due to the lack of early mother love, she had a sadness in her even when she sang, which made her voice sound as though she were crying. Marilyn Monroe, too, had been unloved. In the end, she had died of loneliness, since no one really understood how soft and sensitive she was. They just used her talents and beauty to make themselves feel better. Even these celestial beings suffered "secret agonies" and "unlawful desires." This all made so much sense to me. (Due to Jewish history, my life was full of agony; due to the Torah, my desires would often qualify as unlawful.) I wrapped the stars' secret agonies and unlawful desires around me like a warm, familial hug. It was delicious to go below the obvious first layer of things.

Here—before ever picking up a novel or seeing a play— I learned my first lessons in character and plot: "The Man Who Makes Marilyn Forget the Hard Times"; "Sophia: 'A Baby Would Complete Me.'" From these precious periodicals, I extended my limited English glossary: "torrid," "madly," "estrangement," "attempted suicide," "bombshell." "Raven-haired temptress" was an adjectival phrase that especially drew black-haired me. Such creatures were always dark and mysterious; they knew how to come out of a shadow and light up a smoke—preferably at the end of an elegant holder.

In these periodicals, moreover, the Hair Wars were openly reported, scored, and analyzed. My mother, for example, favored Debbie Reynolds, a sunny, perky blonde. Debbie was "unsinkable," a Doris and Betty–like good and spunky girl next door. When she lost her cheating husband to Elizabeth Taylor, it was obviously because Elizabeth was a "raven-haired temptress." Liz and Eddie married at Grossinger's

Country Club, in the Borscht Belt, the summer refuge in the Catskill Mountains where Jews annually went in search of fresh air. I was proud to be associated with such drama. My sultry idol had even converted to the laws of Abraham and his wife and helpmeet, Sarah.

My mother may have "tsk'd" and tutted over Elizabeth Taylor, but, like everyone else, she could not get enough of this irresistible vixen with drives of her own. It is here, during the Reynolds-Taylor standoff, that my mother began to buy up all the magazines on the stand; together, we hungrily devoured them. Did I ever ask my mother to explicate the hair-color valences of this story? Did I ever say, "Could *this* raven-haired temptress have been saved? Would the Nazis have hated her, too?" To my mother, this was just a game. To me, it was a growing obsession, if not a strategy. One day, I would venture out and save the Jews.

I did not discuss these plans with my mother, since she considered all non-Jewish males to be not only forbidden but beneath desiring.

"But you love Jimmy Stewart!" I'd protest, noticing how her little feet wiggled around on the bed as we watched his old movies, sometimes appearing to nod, "Yes, Jimmeleh, yes." I think she liked his gentleness, his hemming and hawing—so unlike my father's strong and dictatorial machismo.

"Feh! That is not real! I could never love a goy who drinks and calls me a dirty Jew!"

"But Jimmy Stewart would never—"

"Feh. He would. This person I see on the television is just a character. A fantasy."

Not to me. Retreating back to my Archie books, I developed my own romantic theories. Archie obviously preferred Veronica to Betty. The names themselves would tell you that. Elizabeth would survive, she would shine on like the stars in heaven. Yes, she would have her tracheotomy, her pneumonia; her beloved Mike Todd would perish in a fiery plane crash, husbands would bore her (and in later years, I learned, she'd even bloat), but she would live, live, live! I could be Sonia, then, not Susie, after all.

Sonia, Sonia, Sonia . . . Exotic temptress-to-be of Washington Heights.

I was also mesmerized when Elizabeth *dropped* Debbie's husband, moving on to the primal, Welsh Celt Richard Burton. Wearing a glossy, ropy black wig, she played Cleopatra, who seduces Caesar, then Antony. Entire empires would be vanquished as she yawned and stretched. When the married Burton would refuse to divorce his wife, Elizabeth/Cleopatra would checkmate with a suicide attempt. She could not live without him—and he would relent, helpless in the force of her passion. The Vatican screamed. The world exploded. Amazing sex was doubtless had. Or, as I saw it at the time, a long, long, long kiss.

Moral: Blondes did *not* necessarily have more fun! As I grew older, I swore, I would fully investigate this thesis.

La Vie en Rose

JEWS COULD HAVE FUN, too, even death camp graduates. There could even be mad sexual sparks. Simon had fallen in love with my mother in the course of one lovely winter's evening. He was handsome, with an athletic body and a refined face. There they were, fellow survivors, not only both from Lithuania, but from the Kovno area. He had survived Dachau, where my mother's father had lost his life. And she had survived Stutthof, where his mother had lost hers.

They met at a Lithuanian Jewish Survivors' Ball in New York, shortly after they had both arrived, he alone, she, with her widowed mother, Liba. Gita Davidow Wery-Bey was elegant and pretty, fragrant and soft-spoken; Simon was poetic, intense, virile. In that old-world ballroom at a once-elegant hotel, they danced as though nothing could vanquish their private music. Now they were in the land of promises and freedom. Arms surrounding each other, palms clasped, they were a miracle of motion. Their song was Edith Piaf's bittersweet, knowing "La Vie en Rose." Despite all that had happened to them, a life in pink—all of it soft and sweet and fragrant—could be wished for. They shared this dream as they glided across the floor, dancing sweeping Viennese waltzes and nimble fox trots. When a polka was played, she flew in his arms, in circles and circles of hope.

While noting that Simon was "merely" a craftsman, and though some who knew him said he had a terrible temper, my grandmother liked her daughter's suitor. Simon was gallant and respectful to Liba, promising that she could live with him and her daughter forever. After a few more dates, during which he was charming, and she shy and receptive, Gita agreed to marry Simon. Until the end of their lives they loved "La Vie en Rose," and always danced together beautifully, as though—in some fairy tale in which nothing else impinges—they had been made for each other. Sometimes, on a wintry New York Sunday, they even ice-skated together in Central Park, he guiding her through routines both forward and backward. Still, much was to detract from their harmony. The dark and Heathcliffian man she married bore no relation to her kind, gentle father.

Menachem Mendel Wery-Bey, my maternal grandfather, was a prosperous gentleman with "a neat blonde moustache and cornflower-blue eyes," my mother would say, with an odd touch of pride. "No one could ever tell he was Jewish." She often retold a story about his encounter with a German SS officer. Wearing the yellow cloth star all Jews had been forced, by Third Reich law, to wear, he'd been stopped while walking in the street, or rather, the gutter, as Jews had been pushed off the pavement.

"You! Dirty Jew!"

He had turned around and swept off his homburg. Seeing my grandfather's pale blonde hair, parted neatly

in the middle, and staring into his pale eyes, the SS officer had softened and said:

"Here! Really! Are you truly a Jew?"

And my mother told me that her father had answered
without hesitation: "Yes. I am a Jew."

In the hierarchy of heaven, this was the highest form of
nobility. He had acted *al kiddush Hashem*—to sanctify God's
name. While of course it was permissible for those who could
to hide their Jewishness—all rabbis agreeing that nearly anything was permissible in order to save a life—this avowal was
the heroic approach. Simply to stand in the gutter, wearing
a yellow star, and affirm—given a chance to deny it—that
one was a Jew, faithfully following the commandments, was
a mitzvah, and showed a man's sense of principle.

"A filthy rodent Jew?" shouted the Nazi, grabbing his la-
pel, smiling, a gleeful hound finally grabbing his little fox.
He wrapped his free arm around my grandfather's neck,
and, bending him in half, dragged him over to a nearby
trough ("for horses," my mother explained, "so they should
drink"). The Nazi forced Menachem Mendel's head into
the water, pushing it down as far as he could. My grandfather nearly drowned. Finally, he let him up for air, and
asked him:

"And now. Did the water clean you? Or are you still a
dirty Jew?"

Barely able to breathe, my grandfather nodded his head,
yes.

"What 'Yes'? You're clean? Or you're a dirty Jew?"

"I am . . ." he gasped, ". . . Jewish." *Yiddish* was the word he
used, a word full of tenderness when spoken by Jews.

Jude was the word the Germans used, the word embla-
zoned on the yellow star. *Yoo-deh.* Didn't they know the word

was based on the people and land of Judah? The insignia of the tribe of Judah was a lion, rampant! Our word for Jew was *Yehudi*, and my middle name, Judith, or *Yehudit*, in its original Hebrew, was not an insult, but a badge. It meant Jewess, a woman from the tribe of Judah. A lioness. A warrior. Maybe, I wondered, everyone couldn't deal with this kind of history. We had lived in what was known as the Holy Land. Our name was Israel, Judah, Judea. We once had a kingdom; Jerusalem was our center. These were powerful things. The Bible itself—and most everyone seemed to believe in it—said we were chosen by God. Were our enemies jealous that we were teacher's pet? Did everyone want to be the "special one"? Was this why Snow White's stepmother, that usurper, wanted her step-daughter's heart cut out in the woods—so she, the Queen, could for once be "the fairest"? The Nazis liked to consider themselves a "Master Race." Was this simply sibling rivalry, like madman Cain killing gentle Abel, like Joseph's big brothers throwing him down into the pit? And did we have to keep playing this game?

OK—you win! *You're* chosen! Or as we used to say in the playground—"You're It!" That meant that everyone would now chase *you*. Good luck with that! As for us, could we say "Not It"—and be safe?

What a relief that would be—to be treated as normal, neither predator nor prey. My grandfather was a middle-aged bourgeois with a well-groomed mustache. He just wanted to get back to his family. He wasn't hurting anyone. He had never hurt anyone. He wasn't even that religious—and whom would it have hurt if he had been?

But the Jews were "it" that day, and so his head was shoved back underwater, a sick baptism of hatred. My father told me that Europe's Christians had blamed the Jews for everything from poisoning their wells, to causing the Black Plague, to drinking the blood of Christian children (Jews were thought to "need" this blood for their Passover matzohs). Didn't anyone know that Jews are forbidden to taste blood at all, that this clear injunction can easily be found in our mutually beloved Bible? Did they really think Jesus had eaten unleavened *child-blood* bread at his Last Supper—a Passover meal called a seder? Why, if they worshipped him so much, did they attack the religion he'd followed?

As a child, my father would avoid the churches as they let out on Easter Sunday. After hearing about the death of their Lord, mobs of screaming boys would chase him, screaming, "Blood Drinker! Christ Killer! Child Murderer!" Their parents, the women wearing crosses, would watch and do nothing. But it was Simon's father, who had a grain mill, a wife, and three small children, who had been murdered, and these very mobs, screaming boys later grown to dangerous men, would jeer and shove as he and his widowed mother were carted off on their via dolorosa to the death camps.

"My Papa came home that night," my mother continued. "He was nearly dead from being so much in that water. He couldn't speak. Later, he told us, with a voice that was breaking:

"'They asked me if I was a Jew. I told them. I will tell them this even if they kill me.'"

"And he did," she said, "and they did."

My grandfather's younger brother David took another route. Apparently, he looked even more like an "Aryan" than my grandfather did. Granduncle David had a long, handsome and strong-boned face, flaxen hair, and pale blue eyes. His nerves may well have been as steely as those of an SS officer. Passing as a Christian, he hid in plain sight, walking boldly on the pavements of Kovno, no yellow star to mark him. He married a Catholic woman and had children of his own, baptized—for their own safety—into his wife's religion. David eventually died of pneumonia in a hospital, in a bed with clean white sheets, under a cross nailed to the wall over his head, nursed by compassionate sisters. He was buried in a Christian graveyard. My mother never talked about him, or his wife and children—her aunt and first cousins. I found out about them only when I was grown, with children of my own.

"Saving your life like that, I don't know," she said. "I can't judge him. But his family—no one knows they were Jews. Thousands of years of history, lost." Not for the first time, I thought: Ignorance *can* be bliss.

Then she said: "Sonialeh. Do you think I know all the answers? Maybe he did the right thing. But my father was a proud Jew—and now we talk about him. We honor him. Right? I lived, I had you and your brother, and you will remember who we are and what we stood for. Your children will have a soul full of precious history. Knowing who you are, where you come from, that's a reason to live. About my uncle David, what can we say? Did that person even exist?"

His family lives in Las Vegas now, most of them croupiers. It thrills me to think of them sometimes, my kin safe amidst that anonymous dazzle of a timeless (clockless) world. And then again, without the known history, without the weight of time—are they really my true kin?

The Almost Blind Watchmaker

IT WAS GROWING HARDER for my father to put life into his timepieces. He'd wind them regularly, keys held by his dexterous but increasingly thick fingers. He had acquired a rare brain disorder in America—acromegaly, a pituitary tumor that gradually, almost imperceptibly, caused his face to change, coarsening his features until he was nearly unrecognizable. Slowly, his feet widened and his fingers broadened. As his jaw grew, his perfect, white teeth began to splay and his straight nose became bulbous. From a handsome man, he became a giant trapped in a too-small frame.

When I played with my skinny, angular Barbie doll, I began to use another doll—not Ken, but a baby doll, all rolls and sausage-like extremities—to play the man, the husband. Both this doll and my father were bald, which added to the feeling that he was a circus strongman, a sideshow, perhaps, but formidable and forbidding. Had a doctor not diagnosed his illness, my father would have eventually gone blind. When he told me this, I dreamed repeatedly of his poor right eye, the one that held the loupe, sightless. And the poor loupe, with no eye to see into the truth of a ticking world. And the poor clocks, forever to be broken, heartbroken. And the world unfixed. A quick operation removed the tumor, however, and my father's sight was saved.

On the other hand, the damage to my father's appearance was permanent.

I realized, as his face grew, that my hopes of having a normal, conventional life *in any sense* were close to nil. His voice deepened, becoming darker and more sepulchral. When he answered the doorbell or the phone, he sounded like Lurch, the Frankensteinian butler from the *Addams Family* TV show.

"WHO IS DIS?" he would rumble, like a giant saying "Fee, Fie, Fo, Fum."

Sabbath brought a change to everything. Simon never worked on that day, and the importunate ticking of clocks (like the ravages of illness) was ignored. Instead, the synagogue became my father's sanctuary. He would arrive as soon as the doors opened and take his seat on the corner of a long wooden bench, a silken, white prayer shawl draping his shoulders, its case lying next to him to save my brother's seat. An hour or so after the services started, my mother would appear with Manny and me. She and I would take our seats in the women's section, high above the men's. My brother would slide in near his father, who would show him the place in the prayer book, then sink back into his own devotions.

My mother and I could hardly see them from our aerie near the brass chandeliers. During most of the service, in fact, the women talked amongst themselves, picking up important information about one another's children, their struggles and beaming accomplishments. I loved to listen to the gossip, sniffing my mother's Arpège off her silk scarves, playing with her rings and her bracelets (often borrowed from the store's showcases). My mother would happily slip off these treasures, shining them on her embroidered hand-kerchiefs and putting them on my own hands and wrists. The women's service was in its way as restorative as the men's. It was cozy to sniff our perfumes and jingle our charms, cozy to hear words of satisfaction whispered in Yiddish behind hard-working hands, now at leisure.

My father prayed with a deep intention, which the Or-thodox call *kavanah*. It was the same deep intensity that he gave to the fixing of watches, but in prayer he appealed to the single and limitless heart of God. As he sang along with the congregation to the old melodies, Simon's voice soared. He had always had an operatic skill, and though untrained, his voice could carry a heartbreaking vibrato. If anything, subtle new depths in its timbre gave it a richer, more prophetic sound as he rose to the bimah and chanted the Torah's verses to the notes of ancient cantillation. The holy, hopeful words rose to the heights of our little sanctu-ary, trailing into the women's section, vibrating off the brass chandeliers that hung from the ceiling, sailing into my ears.

A big "shhhhh" would travel through the congregation— and even our homey ring of chatter would become still. And then we'd hear a massive voice, disembodied, echoing through the congregation and somehow transforming it. So serious, the words, the voice, the source, and that collec-tive, reverberative hush. I'd almost be relieved when it was over, and my father would return to the world as he always was, standing near me to take his little paper cup of wine as other men clapped him on the back to congratulate him or solemnly shook his hand.

"Yesher koach" they would say. Extra strength, or More power to you.

It did not matter then that his speaking voice was a shade too deep, or his fingers too thick. From his early childhood, Simon had had no father, but God was his father, and he had sung to him. And the men had surrounded him and blessed his strength, even after the pituitary tumor that had almost felled him.

My father never complained about his malady, or his appearance. He would laugh about his looks, which I found charming and heroic:

"I wonder if I am the handsomest man in New York now," he'd say, or, less facetiously, "I know it sounds ridiculous, but I used to be quite a nice-looking fellow." He kept a picture on the dresser from years past; he had looked like an old-fashioned movie star before I ever got to know him.

His massive hands, about which people sometimes remarked, were still gentle and deft. His eyes, which had almost been blinded by the growing pituitary bearing down on the optic nerve, saw deeply, and radiated innocence, honesty, and wisdom. They were still handsome, set off by his dark, expressive eyebrows.

I loved my father through and through. In his absence, I felt unknown and unseen. Even when he sang in the synagogue, I was removed from him, exiled in the women's section, apart. But there were times when my father entered my world, took his loupe out, shed the prayer shawl, and pulled me toward him. My joy was boundless—I had been "selected." Only then, chosen, did I feel fully alive.

It was my father who would make my bland food palatable. On special occasions, he would make me neat, yummy omelets, the way I liked them—the eggs anything but soft and runny. He would cut thin slices of potatoes and make crisp fries for me, slice cucumbers and lay them down in sandwiches with thick brown bread and butter. He was deft with a knife, and could slice potato finely, pare an apple peel into one long circle, drop M&M's into my farina bowl without my noticing, one by one, making them appear to pop out of the gray sludge, a bit of sweet hope and color.

He would also tuck me in at night, tight, like a mummy, which I loved—the covers tucked even under me, so that I felt snug and safe. Then he would call me by a pet name: Karaputzi. He told me it was a Slavic slang word meaning "cute little child." I liked the sound of it. When I was sick with the croup, it was he who would stay with me all night, leading me from my bed into a bathroom steaming with vapors from the shower, waving the mist toward my mouth. At moments like this, as when he fixed watches, he was infinitely patient—and I felt loved.

If I awoke in the middle of the night and called out for him: "I'm scared of this darkness, Daddy," he would say, "Read the bedtime Sh'ma." The Sh'ma is the prayer all Jews know, attesting to the oneness of God. "Hear O Israel, Adonai is our God, Adonai is one." These words may have comforted me, but more comforting was the man who tucked me in again, assuring me that I was safe in the world, no matter what had happened in the past, or what time it now was.

Still, it was hard for me to sustain that feeling of safety when the real world was so fragmented, not just Jews and non-Jews but my father's doting love for his Karaputzi, and the more conditional appreciation he felt for my "specialness." It was possible to please him, and it was also possible to deeply disappoint him.

"God has given you something extra," he'd say, "and these gifts have been there from the moment you were born. I could see them from the moment I first saw you. *You* are going to be a great lady."

These words were like an official coronation, with the accompanying sense of responsibility. I was required to do my share, under my father's watchful approval. He would witness my deeds and affirm my extra-chosenness. Heavy is the head that wears the crown that a wounded, moody father imposes on his child. And such tributes, focused on a scrawny, black-haired daughter, would cause my mother to tighten her lips and show me her rare cold side. It didn't help when, during a marital argument, her husband would drag me into it and draw a virtual bull's-eye on me:

"Gita! What took me ten hours to explain to you—and I still don't think you will ever understand it—this little girl, this *klayne maydel*, she understood it in the very first minute!"

It probably also didn't help that these praiseful words made me beam, like the desperate, foolish child I was.

He even liked my dark hair, which came from his dark, intense side of the family. The original Sonia Taitz had been beautiful, he told me, with black hair and deep, blue-green eyes. When I'd wish for blondeness, he'd remind me that I had a special beauty, an ancient Jewish charm. He comforted me with tales of dark, exotic beauties such as Queen Esther, who, long ago in Persia, had won a beauty contest, married a king, and saved her people. He assured me that dark eyes and hair were rare and desirable. In Lithuania, he told me, as in Poland or Russia, any peasant could produce a crop of illiterate towheads with dumb pale eyes that understood nothing.

So, like my paternal grandmother, I was a Snow White in coloring, and my mother was already showing a slight tendency toward the stepmother side. Who could blame her? It wasn't some magic mirror saying that I was the fairest of them all—it was my father, her own husband, her man.

Piano and Potatoes

MY MOTHER'S EYES were spring-green, cat-green, her round cheeks pink as a Dresden doll's, her nose dotted with small freckles. While my father had an ageless old man's demeanor (not only Yul Brynner, but Zorba, or the later Picasso), Gita remained dewy, fragrant, and unlined throughout her life. Her favorite color scheme, and it suited her, was "flowers"—any color, all colors. They blossomed on her sheets, in her dresses, in vases all over the house, on the towels and paper napkins. Her hands were soft, but there was ready power and capability in them from her years of practicing the piano. She had lived in the pretty Lithuanian town of Kovno, practicing her Bach inventions and Hanon exercises and arpeggios in a stately redbrick home overlooking the river. Her duplex had large French windows opening out onto the treetops, and on the ground floor of this building, which he owned, was her father's little department store, right across from the university.

Chopin was my mother's most beloved composer, and although she was seemingly not fiery herself, his notes flew out of her body and transformed her, and everything around her, into a magic tapestry of passions, tears, dashed hopes, and soaring emotional resurrection. In Europe, my mother had practiced and given recitals on concert grand pianos; in Washington Heights, she played on a carved mahogany upright with creamy ivory keys. At four, I began pressing down on those keys, my mother's fingers on top of mine. Later, my mother found me a teacher from Juilliard who had been trained by the legendary Madame Rosina Lhévinne (of the Moscow Conservatory). After a short audition, Mrs. Ruskin said I was promising, but I shied away from the piano and rarely practiced, and thus never arrived beyond the "Für Elise" and sonatina stage. I preferred a subsidiary role, taking solace from the world my mother could create out of sound.

Each week, my mother would drag me to this teacher, who lived beside the Hudson River in a poorer neighborhood about twenty blocks south of our own. Mrs. Ruskin's life was music. She had raised her son to become a concert pianist, and her small apartment was filled with grand pianos. One, with silent keys, fascinated me especially.

"That's so that her boy could even practice during the night," my mother whispered to me. "Even I never had such a thing back in Europe."

During my lessons, my poor, devoted teacher made brilliant notations all over my music sheets or demonstrated concepts like the diminuendo with her capable hands. I focused mostly on the fact that she shaved her arms, leaving a rough stubble that I could feel when she slid her arms under mine to give me the sense of an arpeggio sweep. While Mrs. Ruskin would scribble endless tips in my spiraled workbook, I took the opportunity to daydream, my mouth watering from the hamburgers that Mr. Ruskin always seemed to be frying.

My mother, meanwhile, sat just to my left, on a wooden adjustable stool like mine, enraptured by the lesson. After my hour was over, she would stay with Mrs. Ruskin as I escaped to the living room to better inhale hamburger smells or play a muted chord on her son's silent practice piano. From there, I would hear my mother's music emerge from the lesson room, rich and strong. Sometimes her notes were followed by a pause, a conversation, Mrs. Ruskin's suggested phrasing, and then the improvement, coming from my mother's own powerful hands—and making all the difference. Her melodies could soar without the use of crescendo; they could get right into you and make you forget this world. It never occurred to me then to mourn my mother's lost career as a performer. I never let her guide my practice on the piano back home, which I balked and avoided. My increasingly detailed assignments, including the awful Hanon exercises, became more and more tedious to me.

Instead, I waited for the times when my mother would make her own music come to life. I sat below her, watching her delicate, small feet on the pedals create gorgeous diapasons of weeping notes that soared and reverberated until the world disappeared and all that existed was the world's one great soul, yearning. Safe under the keyboard of the heavy old Knabe, I felt my eyes fill with welcome tears. I felt rich, full, and satisfied, surrounded with jewel-like tones that matched my glistening, teary, rainbowized world, sounds that never ended but were sustained by her pedaling. There was no place I felt happier as a child than by the feet of my soft, pretty, and talented mother, the quintessence of all that was fruitful and giving and female. I felt all of the best of Europe there, the fairy-tale palaces, the delicate cakes I had sampled at the bakery, with names like Linzer, and

Sacher, Black Forest and Napoleon. Something in the old wood of this piano, something in the yellow Schirmer book of Chopin, something in the language of music itself hinted at these lost but not forgotten worlds.

My mother's hands smelled of Camay soap, and the cameo etched into the bars looked like her, as did the bonneted, bonny lady on the Sun-Maid raisin box, joyous in her native vineyard. In the kitchen, however, Gita took on the savory soul of onions, potatoes, bay leaves, and dill. She would sit at the round table with her mother, humming as she pared, peeled, and chopped. Sometimes, she would take a heavy, metal meat grinder and send beef out in curling pink ribbons, which she formed into her *klops* and her *galuptzie.* From early morning, pots would clang as she dragged them out, a cacophony of metal, from under and over the sink.

On weekends, my mother would cook enough for an entire week, boiling chickens and chopping liver, hacking iceberg lettuce and tomatoes into sturdy wedges. She would make great vats of chicken soup, of which she jarred large portions for her housebound neighbor Mrs. Shroodel. My grandmother might be shelling peas alongside, and if I went into the kitchen, one or the other of them would offer me some *arbeslach.*

"Vilst du doch essen?" So, do you want to eat?

I was a mouth to be fed for the both of them. If I said "no," they often looked stricken, and one or the other might say:

"Someone's life could have been saved from such good food."

"But she doesn't eat it." They often talked like this, to

each other, over my head, about me. Shelling the peas, shaking their heads, philosophical, disappointed.

"Spoiled."

They saw that my father thought I was special, perhaps too special to be part of the kitchen crew. They saw how he favored and selected me, the little dark latecomer, over my older brother and them.

"You give her something so good, and she turns her face from it."

When they talked about saving lives from starvation, they were not referring to the proverbial, oft-imagined, starving children in India or Africa. They meant real people, people they knew and remembered, perhaps even my own dying blood relatives. They had seen children like me starving during the war. The least I could do was be grateful.

So they persisted, holding a handful of hard peas or a juicy slice of tomato to my mouth, and eventually I'd share in the game by accepting the life-saving food, nibbling it from their palms like a small rooting animal.

Veal in Love

IN MY EARLIEST YEARS I was raised like a condemned veal calf: restricted activity, sunless in my crate, muscles kept weak, tender, and white. But there actually were times that I got out of the house. The problem was that I got out with my grandmother, who was so afraid I'd run away (or run at all) that she kept me on a leash. Actually, it was a harness that wrapped around my shoulders and belted around my waist like the top of some wonderful lederhosen ensemble. On the other end was Bubbe, who liked to sit on the bench right outside the gated "water sprinkler area" in the park. I was tethered to her in the heat as the other children, primarily Irish, ran barefoot in their underwear beneath the cold sprays.

My grandmother wore dark, loose-fitting dresses with a narrow little belt of the same fabric, suggesting the latitude where her waist had once been. She was neither fat nor round, but staunch and distinguished, with the stolid, unmovable air of an Indian chief in an old daguerreotype. Her wispy hair surrounded a strong, tragic face with high, dignified cheekbones and thin, unimpressable lips. Bubbe was grim in her task of keeping me from all harm, and harm began at the door of our apartment. When I look at it now, the playground she took me to seems mild and tame. In my childhood, I saw it through her eyes, as a wilderness full of naked savages (the "other" children, the "gentile" children), mountains (a little rock formation where my brother used to climb, out of her line of sight, free as a goat in Heidi's Alpine wonderland), some metal swings, a sprinkler area, monkey bars and a couple of seesaws. Our poor little grandma was tired and sad and old. My mother often told me that she had been happy and game before the war, that she had had a beautiful voice and sang well. There was a picture, from much later, of my grandmother laughing, as she and mother rowed a boat together. For years and years I thought this was how they had come to America. And I thought that that was the last time she really enjoyed herself, side by side with her daughter, rowing to freedom (they were actually on the lake in Central Park).

To me, Bubbe was someone who wore boxy brown old-lady shoes, tying up the sides with assertive laces. I wonder now—when did grandmothers stop wearing this uniform? It must have been relaxing, in those days, to be permitted to give up so thoroughly, to simply surrender to softness, comfort, and anonymity. My Bubbe, like many others, wore dark colors, those amazing shoes (they must have been reassuring, a solid, yet soft, base for her on earth), a *tichel* covering her head on colder days. The grandma palette contained nothing but soothing browns, grays, and nearly black navy blues. Fabrics tended toward the tweedy and fuzzy. Buttons were large and often interesting. Cardigans were de rigeuer. In the rain, Bubbe would pull out a polka-dotted, plastic version of her kerchief. She wore no makeup, and over her regal bones the skin was soft and scored with majestic wrinkles, suggesting vast knowledge which no child could understand. In her bag, which closed with a large metal clasp, she carried no lipstick, no mirror—just a little money and a white, embroidered handkerchief with which, in the summer, she dabbed moisture off her face, or wiped the ambient dirt off mine.

I wore little white socks with lacy edges, and well-polished, sturdy white shoes of the type immortalized in brass on many a mantel. I wore a stiff cotton dress with a ruffled petticoat underneath, and a cardigan with embroidered flowers and pearly buttons. But I had eyes, and I could see something I liked. There they were—children playing gleefully. These were our neighbors, fellow immigrants' kids, with runny noses, scabs on their knees, dirt under their nails. They suggested a wild, unbridled freedom—the freedom to hurt, to be hurt, to soar, to fall, to laugh and splash and be crazy. Two of these, a pair of twin sisters, used to come up to me sometimes; their clear blue eyes and crazy orange hair amazed me.

"Hey, I'm Loretta!"

"Hey, and I'm Charlotte!"

"Whycome you can't play?"

"And whycome you don't talk?"

"Who's that lady, your great-granny or somethin'?"

Long pause for staring.

"Doncha wanna get wet?"

Oh, yes. Yes. I did want to get wet, muddy, and wild. All that spoke of the world outside, the world that increasingly drew me. But what was I to do, tethered (literally) to my elders, who feared wildness in both its natural and human forms, who could take a chicken and boil it to whiteness and serve it with limp, exhausted vegetables and a fifty-pound potato kugel, thus stopping all impulses to sense, to lust, to budge? And how could I explain all this, when the only language I could speak was Yiddish—forged from millennia of exile from my own precious, base nature?

Bubbe spoke for both of us. Grudgingly, she opened her mouth and muttered: "Gey aveck, du vilde chayes!" (Go away, you wild beasts!) Not looking at them, she would make shooing motions with her hands, as though to say, "Why do they keep tormenting us, these goyim; what do they want from us now? Does it hurt them to see us alive, in one piece, resting and enjoying the sun? Or do they want to help us break our bones?"

Loretta and Charlotte did not speak Yiddish, but they understood. Looking back, it is more than likely that their fathers and uncles were the very men who came into our buildings and fixed the boilers and the water pipes. I am sure there was plenty of Yiddish in their lives in that neighborhood. After staring some more at both of us, pityingly, without hostility, searchingly, the girls would resume their wild, wet frolics.

And I would be left alone again, to look at Billy.

Billy was the one who rode the faucets—rode them, I tell you. I did not have the vocabulary yet, but this was Nietzchean, primal, anarchic, audacious.

Shall I compare him to a stormy day? Was my image of my people so set already, with the idea of "trouble"—in the form of chaos, pogroms, machismo, already counterpoised? No Jewish boy would ride the faucets like that. They wore yarmulkas and glasses, and sounded out the ancient letters, their heads buried in books (literally; the way to study was literally to hunch over a holy book and bury your head between its hard, embossed covers as though making a brain-sandwich with God at the center). But my father had a streak of this wildness in him, in his temper and in his vaunted exploits of the past.

And Billy had this streak of wildness that I can now unabashedly term *goyish*. The word *goy*, so often misunderstood, literally means "nation." It comes from the Bible—and it simply means the nations of the world. Jews are goyim too, in that sense. But in my book, it will always mean "free of restraint and free of pain." We Jews can fake it, but no one who has been touched by the Holocaust, my father and myself included, can actually and consistently make it. We are too sad, too worried and exquisitely broken into facets.

Billy would sit on the fountain spigots and water would spray from all directions, its power nearly blowing him off, but no, like a mad rodeo star he'd maintain his seat, squashing down the waters that would nonetheless rise around him in a cloud of mist and power.

This boy's eyes were smudgy and blue, even the lids seeming dirty, narrowed, full of the smoke of the cigarettes that he would likely pick up within a few years. There was a sense of pale fire within, a virile appraisal and direct approach to the game. Thor with a thunderbolt, all of six years old. His knees were covered with scabs, his chest visible under his pathetic thin and sleeveless undershirt, his lean arms already muscled. He was barefoot, of course he was, barefoot with large flat feet that splashed through the water and got where they needed to go. How did I know his name? Everyone was shouting it, especially the other boys; he was the alpha male of the Washington Heights (at 173rd Street) playground sprinkler.

I needed Billy, I wanted Billy; he would be the antidote

for me. If I was the José of the picture, the Ricky Ricardo, Billy could provide the American ballast to my untoward exoticism.

I wished to see Billy's name, along with mine, on that luminous Desilu pillow. Wild Billy—the exquisite, dirt-covered boy in my playground. I chased him around once—got free of my Bubbe and chased him. He stopped running away, then came at me and threw me down abruptly, shoving dirt by the handful into my mouth. I was totally shocked, but glad of the information. Billy had talked to me in his own language. It was foreign to my poignant Yiddish, and even his dirt had the taste of life in it.

ALL MOTHERS WORRY about their children, but mine must have been uniquely afraid of losing me or my brother to some sudden tragedy, and uniquely aware that such disasters could, and did, occur.

As a small child, I kept getting cold after cold, bronchitis, fevers, croup, and chronic tonsillitis. I remember my doctor, a twinkling Jewish immigrant from Germany, coming regularly to see me. Dr. Hershowitz was an old-world gentleman, patient, genteel, and kind. Though he was a pediatrician, he himself was childless. When I visited his home office, his wife, a stout, middle-aged woman with yellow-blonde hair and piercing blue eyes would lead me into a waiting room that held a birdcage of canaries. Having little birds was very Mittel-European, very bourgeois. Though their apartment was as small as my own, and the "waiting room" really a dark foyer, I could envision the large, airy sitting room in Frankfurt where Dr. and Mrs. Hershowitz may once have served tea and cakes, as their canaries twittered by sunny French windows.

"See my Fritzl sing to my Dietzl," Frau Hershowitz would say, or something to that effect. (I always wanted to laugh, but she was dead serious about those fragile birds, who, even when dead and replaced, were always named Fritzl and Dietzl.) After listening to the songbirds, I'd take a seat on a tiny little chair by a tiny little table and take a comic book down from a shelf. All the comics were Disney, and all were about the Duck family. I especially loved reading about Daisy, who wore elegant shoes and screamed hysterically at Donald. It seemed a good turn-about, so unlike the situation in my own home, where no one dared talk back to my father, much less raise their voice to him.

When I was really sick, Dr. Hershowitz would pay a house call, carrying a heavy leather black bag that closed on top with a big brass snap. Out of it would come his large rubbery stethoscope. The old doctor would meticulously insert the earpieces and, after asking me to lift my pajama top, hoist a cold metal disk to my chest. In German (which I somehow instantly understood), he would ask me to breath hard and to cough. Removing the earpieces slowly, the doctor would then shake his head dramatically at my mother, eyes raised to meet her consternation. Sitting on the edge of my bed with folded hands, he would say:

"Sie ist echt krank." She is truly ill.

The language was remarkably like Yiddish. But there was a formality to it, a tightness of the lips and tongue, which made it seem as though stern things were being spoken of, and in this case they were.

"Echt krank?" My mother would answer with her own perfect German accent, of which I could see she was proud. She seemed transformed from her Yiddisheh Mama self when she spoke like that. There was a layer of her that was of course concerned about the sickness being discussed, and another in which she was a lady, educated and well-postured, who could converse, any day, along the streets of the Danube or Rhine. After all, she had lived in Germany for years after the war, awaiting her American papers, and even dated a German Jewish doctor, whom, she always noted when telling the tale, drove her around in a convertible. In Germany, my mother apparently was Grace Kelly. Here, however, she was a tired mother with a pale, black-haired daughter who always seemed to have bronchitis, strep, croup, or tonsillitis.

The fact of my illness established, the remedy was applied. "So! Sie must haben die Spritz!"

I understood this dreadful phrase as well. I must have the injection. I must have been *spritzed* once or twice a season. Even today, when I hear a word with a similar root applied— "spritz" or white wine "spritzer," my buttocks clench in miserable anticipation of the needle with which Dr. Hershowitz would puncture my sad little tush in my earliest years.

Then, one day, when I was four and a half, a big change occurred. No more visits to Fritzl and Dietzl, no more housecalls from Herr Doktor. Instead, the morning began differently than any other in the past. What I first noticed was that my mother had a manic edge about her. She was letting me skip kindergarten, which I'd recently begun; she was smiling and laughing. She was talking loudly and fast about taking me to the toy store on Amsterdam Avenue, the one from whose window she always pulled me away.

There were few store-bought toys in my life and my brother's. My parents struggled to support us, and playthings were not a top priority. Mostly, we made do with marbles and pink rubber balls named Spaldings (we called them Spaldeens). My brother and his friends spent a lot of time melting crayons into bottle caps to play a street game like marbles, called Skully. They also used broomsticks, which, combined with a Spaldeen, made a ball game on our block. We both had our own small boxes of crayons—a single line of eight. But I knew there were more colors, and better toys, somewhere out there.

On this special day, my mother told me that we were going to the toy store, and that I could get *anything I wanted*.

"You mean—can I have Patty Playpal?" This was a doll, advertised nonstop on television, that was three feet tall. If you held her by the arm, Patty would "walk" with you. I wanted her to live in our home. Maybe, sometimes, my parents could tell *her* all about the Holocaust, as I slipped away to join Billy, Loretta, and Charlotte.

"Yeh, sure," she said. "Have a playpal."

"A Betsy Wetsy?" I knew all the great dolls, Chatty Cathy included. There was even one called Tearie Dearie, whose accompanying jingle went like this:

Tearie Dearie, as tiny as can be.
But oh, how she cries—
Cause she needs me.
I wipe my Tearie Dearie's great big eyes,
Cause she's my teary teary teary Tearie Dearie!!!

Disturbing. I had enough "tearie dearies" in my home at the moment. But a big Playpal would be a great friend for me.

And I was bottomless-pit greedy for crayons. I knew that in the world of colors one could go far beyond my little row and have twenty-four, thirty-six, and even—the nirvana of Crayola—the iconic "64 Color" box *with a built-in sharpener*.

"Can I also have a big box of crayons?"

"Sure, yeh, why not."

"I mean the BIG one—the one with *sixty-four* colors, and the sharpener? Can I even have that one?"

Inside that box were colors like blue-violet and violet-blue, red-orange and orange-red—and they were subtly different. There were turquoise and apricot, lilac and magenta; forest green and sea green and olive green; burnt umber and burnt sienna. There was silver and there was gold and there was even copper, which was the subtlest. It spoke of deep-sea treasure, coinage from a lovely mythical realm.

I knew this from my neighbor-friend Esther Plaut's box of sixty-four colors (plus sharpener); at her house, I had juxtaposed all the greens, all the reds, all the yellows, then drawn a flower with each of them, filling the page. If my mother bought me a box, I would make a million flowers for her, who loved them so much.

"Yes, Sonia, you will have all the colors." There was a trace of weariness to her voice. "You will have all the pretty colors you always want."

At this point we started walking into a grand building, bigger than any I had ever seen before. I thought this was the Palace of Toys, a temple for children, perhaps. My mother raced me through revolving doors and into a vast, echoey, and slightly spooky hall. I looked around to see the dolls and teddy bears, the giant Playpals and crying babies, bottles of milk that never ran dry. All I could see were people with grim, set expressions walking quickly in and out. Some were in wheelchairs. Some children were in wheelchairs. The ceilings were high and unfriendly, and emitted a vague, blue, almost underwatery light. Here and there I heard an odd, reverberating shout, and yes, maybe a crying child. A real child, crying in pain. I began to get frightened.

"Okay, now let's go to the crayon part," I said, taking her hand and pulling.

"I'm taking you there," she replied, pulling me the other way.

"Just around the corner? Close by?"

She gripped my hand more tightly and nodded. Her

face was grim, and I wondered why she looked so worried.

"Are you okay, Mommy?"

My mother had two sides to her—90 percent of the time she was sweet, cuddly, approachable, easygoing. The other 10 percent was pinched and tight-lipped, rejecting and refusing. I would see this face more and more when I grew up and broke out of my veal box. And I saw it now.

I remember next waking up in a children's ward, with a throat that felt slashed and bloodied. My eyes were dripping wet. To my left was a wall with a high window. On the sill, unreachable, was a teddy bear that had fallen over on its side. If this was a toy store, it was the toy store from a nightmare. A nurse was trying to shovel melted, yellowish vanilla ice cream into me. I was retching. And my mother was nowhere.

There must have been a moment of sheer horror when she handed me over to the nurses, and later, when they put the gas mask over my face. To this day, I avoid even the haze of steam showers; they remind me of being smothered, as I was that day, with ether. They remind me of my namesake, Sonia, who, like so many women, was led to her death with a lie—that they were going to the showers, and instead were murdered with gas.

Years later, my mother told me that after being discharged from the hospital, I would not eat or speak for the next few days. She told me that she was even more frightened than she had been before the operation to which she had led me. It was bad enough to have had a physically sick child, whom she loved desperately, be taken away for an operation. But my "acting like a crazy" was even more horrifying. My mute hunger strike stopped only when she threatened to take me back to the hospital.

I opened my mouth, finally, and she put some melted ice cream into it.

"Good?" she asked.

"Yes, Mommy," I said, and she smiled, and stroked my hair.

She was the only mother I had, and I continued to need her love, her food, and her good graces. And when I snuggled into her, she felt warm and soft and safe.

I am sorry that I was the daughter whom she had to take to the hospital. The one with the dark hair like Veronica, Elizabeth, and Cleopatra. The one who was so persistently, perversely sick she needed to go to a medical center and have an operation that must have worried her mother to death. The one who, from an early age, craved learning, and what was then the man's world of knowledge and vertical advancement. The one who loved the gold stars and wanted to be special. The one who wanted only to read, and not cook.

I would not sit in the kitchen with her. I would not take the long Shabbat *shpatziers* (walks) with her. All that ever happened on those walks, when I joined her, was that she would introduce me to her friends, trying to show me off—if I would but cooperate.

"Say hello to Mrs. Friedman," she'd say, pushing me forward.

"Hello, Mrs. Friedman," I'd mumble, as my mother adjusted my collar, or tried to tame my messy hair.

I wanted to be different from the world of mothers and daughters, to grow away from what seemed like her female conventionality and subservience and saying hello to Mrs. Friedman on a dull walk in the park. I even hated the fresh air and longed to return to my own world of books and brooding, envisioning a world as good as the one in the television set. Maybe better.

My father's praise seduced me further and further away. The implication of his attentions was that I would be president, Miss America, and a Nobel Prize winner, while my mother toiled in the kitchen, feeding us all with sustaining vats of chicken soup. It was only much later that I understood how important her role was, even later when she herself understood it.

Modern/Orthodox

I NEARLY DIDN'T GO TO YESHIVA, where Torah, myopia, and rounded shoulders became central elements of my childhood. I might have learned more from going to a public school and mixing with all the lucky, scabby children in the neighborhood, like Loretta, Charlotte, and Billy. My father, in fact, had wanted me to become fully a part of American life, to be a typical kid and, at least scholastically, to fit into the melting pot. I attribute this to a sort of idealism that he always had, the sense that all people really did belong together—the same sense that had drawn him happily into the Lithuanian army to march and scale walls like any other young fellow. He was always boasting of how well he could deal with the "outside" world.

For instance, he had no problems befriending all kinds of customers. Watch and clock collectors began coming to see him from every corner of the world, and I'd never seen him happier as his business grew. I'd watch him step away from his workbench to lean over the counter, talking and listening avidly, engrossed. I saw him laughing with a Japanese man; I saw him shaking hands, eyes locking, with a Catholic priest. He found this country, in its very variety, illuminating and liberating, and often said, with a sense of wonder, "Everything and everyone is interesting to me."

I felt the same way. Especially about the goyim.

One time, our superintendent came into the apartment to fix a leak. This is my first recollection of seeing a non-Jew inside. Inside our little chicken-*geshtunken* Jewish home where even the walls were sighing.

I gaped at this hearty Irish immigrant man; I inhaled his essence as though he brought tidings (and a rare curative elixir) from a new planet. Eve herself might have had as big a fascination with the proverbial ripe fruit. Johnny's hair was yellow-orange; his face red, and his button nose large-pored. I stood next to him, as close as I could without tripping him. Watching him lie under the sink (his fawn colored, ankle-high work shoes were scuffed, rubber-soled), then upright and talking (blunt, honest teeth), I agreed with my father's observation that "everything and everyone is interesting."

Actually, my father seemed to find non-Jews even more interesting than Jews. Was it the anthropology? Not entirely. The praise of a non-Jew, or even the feeling he himself felt, of kinship with those outside his beleaguered tribe, made my father feel, finally, chosen. They were the ones who decided most of the fateful events of the world. They were the ones who had allowed him to live. They were the ones whose selection had really counted. To them, he was the chosen of the chosen. And I was the chosen of the chosen of the chosen.

My mother and grandmother, on the other hand, largely closed their minds to the goyish world, which they decided (based on the considerable evidence of their own lives) was wild and shallow in bad and dangerous ways. They felt that as Jews, my brother and I should be educated to be religiously and culturally literate. After all, how many of us were left after the mass murders in Europe? And how many of those were growing up in ignorance, here in America where only the new and modern was revered?

This, too, made sense to my father. Part of him felt that we could never understand history fully, or even the beauty of America, until we appreciated our own heritage. Nothing was sadder to him than Jews by name only, who had no idea why they suffered or sacrificed—no higher ideals to keep them alive spiritually. He regretted having had to leave school so young. His education had been scant, and for the rest of his life he tried to augment it, putting as much energy into the holy books as he did his beloved *Reader's Digest,* with its rousing sense of an improving modernity and of touching human nature.

So I entered first grade at a place called Yeshiva Rabbi Moses Soloveitchik. No, the name alone did not deter my parents from sending both me and my brother to this institution. Indeed, it was not as insular as it sounded: the namesake of the school was a great Lithuanian rabbi who had, not long before, helped usher Modern Orthodoxy into the Jewish world. At first, most yeshivas limited themselves to Jewish studies; they were seminaries that cultivated the scholarly, religious mind and pious practices. Rabbi Soloveitchik, instead, argued that Torah was incomplete without *madah* (science, in the broadest sense). He urged schools to teach all of the world's best knowledge under the same roof. A graduate of such an academy could read both Leviticus and LaFontaine in the original. Such binocular vision could only add to a person's depth perception.

Jewish studies, nonetheless, were paramount at my first school, and children were expected, within months, to speak, read, and write not only in English but in Hebrew. And not just Hebrew, but Biblical Hebrew, and not just Biblical Hebrew, but the semi-cursive notes of the seminal scholar Rashi that annotated each page of the holy texts.

Amidst the rigors of deciphering ancient scripts, I became, like most everyone else in yeshiva, severely nearsighted. It is not as though my scope had ever tended toward the way of the soaring eagles; I had always, anyway, been looking down at my patent-leather Mary Janes, or at the "diamonds" glittering in the pavement they trod. I had closely followed the dust atoms in my parents' bedroom, and had also stared at every floral motif in my bedclothes and pajamas until they revealed pansy-like faces, smiling. As much as I looked at things microscopically, I mulled them as well—the sounds of words, the meaning of slogans on TV, the Desilu heart. I loved the microcosmic, and the intimacy of subtle symbols. As learning Torah often involved decoding each word, phrase, and sentence in multiple ways, I seemed born for it.

I was very happy at Yeshiva Rabbi Moses Soloveitchik. If I was full of questions, this place seemed full of answers, intricate and mystical, as deep as can be. Hebrew sounded delicious to my ears, and oddly familiar. (Indeed, the parts of the Yiddish language that were not based on German came from Hebrew.) This ancient language was rich; it was dark, dense, and chocolaty, and, with just a few words, said everything. For example, a sentence like "I have loved you," with the "you" even being specified as female (as God says to Israel in a tender moment of reassurance), is, in Hebrew, a single word: *Ahavtich*. Its powerful concision was impressive to me even at five, when we began reading the hauntingly beautiful first words of Genesis, or Beraisheet, in its original tongue. The language threw sparks; it did, indeed, feel holy, and a hole was blasted out of the top of my head when I began to learn to read it. Light came in, more light than I had ever experienced before.

The word for light in Hebrew is *or*. It was the main noun in God's first sentence:

"Yehi or." Let there be light.

"Vayehi or." And there was light.

I found every second in school an illuminating alternative to my former life. I loved the piles of prayer books that stood there on the teacher's desk at the beginning of the year—blue-green or magenta, like the Crayola colors—and were passed out to us to keep forever. I loved the brightly colored metallic reward star stickers on the wall, and adding one each day for "effort." I even loved the two-toned walls (beige and forest green) of the hallways and classrooms. The paint was so shiny and clean; the foil stars, which we were allowed to put up ourselves when we earned them, magical. I loved the blackboards, the erasers and sponges that cleaned them, and the teacher's wooden, rubber-tipped pointers (which were used to wake the many drowsy scholars). I loved our school elevator operator, an old gray-haired black gentleman who pulled the iron gates of the Otis closed as we went in—"Single file, shake a leg"—on our way out to recess in a dusty, square yard ringed by chain-link.

I loved running in the yard with the athletic Bunny Milcher, whose American-born parents weren't religious at all, who went to Miami Beach every winter and dove from the high board, and whose main wish in life, unlike mine, was to be "average and happy." I loved her strong legs and arms and thick straight dirty-blonde hair, so unlike the frail and curly haired Esther Plaut.

Most of all, I loved the rabbis, who (like my father) beamed with true joy, a warmth that glowed like pure love, when I (or any other student) grasped some bit of knowledge. We were part of something, together. School was *shul* to me, a synagogue, a temple of magnificence. And the import of it all! Yeshiva was about survival—exiled from country to country, unable for centuries to own land, unsure of loss everywhere, all we had was what we could carry in our heads and hearts. We knew that the verses must be passed on, the traditions kept, the candles lit. The light of knowledge could, without diminishing, illuminate the world, as God had done with his very first words.

Each school day was a Sabbath to me, a paradise (both Hebrew words). Here was a place not only of intellectual illumination, but spiritual rest. My first teacher, Rabbi Lichtiger, used to hug his students. Each morning we went to him, shyly, as we entered the room, for this embrace. His very name, Lichtiger, meant *full of light*, and he held us as though each was a delicate sunbeam banishing darkness, our very beings miracles of survival.

The Holocaust was often on Rabbi Lichtiger's mind. One hushed, snowy day in winter, he told us about his hero, Janusz Korczak, a Jewish teacher in Poland who had been so close to his little students that he had entered the gas chambers with them, despite connections that would have enabled him to be spared. Janusz had refused this help, saying that he could not bear to let his kinderlach, his children, experience any more fear than they had to. He, at least, would not abandon them, and the little that he could do to comfort them, he would.

If Janusz Korczak had raised me, we would have talked about flowers and butterflies, even during the Holocaust. He would not have taken it upon himself to fill my mind with horror, as my parents did, when the Holocaust was actually over. He would not have asked me questions but given me answers. He would have taught me that love is stronger than fear. But just hearing about him gave that concept entry into my mind.

Rabbi Lichtiger was a "Janusz" to me, a safe core within a harsh world. He realized, as my parents sometimes did not, that we were just children, and that nothing was required of us other than to exist, survive, and even enjoy life. Sometimes he gave us candies when we learned an especially hard verse in Hebrew. In the past, we learned, fathers and rebbes used to put honey on their children's fingers as they learned the biblical letters, so that they would forever associate learning with sweetness.

I was also comforted by Rashi, the biblical interpreter. An eleventh century medieval scholar who had lived in France and Germany, Rashi's life had been devoted to a simple yet profound interpretation of the Torah, verse by verse. Without him, many of the passages made no sense. Rashi would explain the meaning beneath these surface mysteries. He was my first literary critic and guide, and I deeply appreciated the role he had taken in life, that of "explainer."

Still, even with his help, the Torah often seemed rigid. Boundaries and opposites seemed to be key themes in traditional Biblical Judaism. When the Sabbath is over, for example, the Havdalah prayer is sung. The word means separation.

Hamavdil bain Kodesh Lechol
(He who separates between the sacred and the profane)
Bain Or Lechoshech
(Between light and darkness)
Bain Yisroel La'amim
(Between Israel and other nations)
Bain Yom Hashvi'i L'Shesheth Yemai Hama'aseh
(Between the Seventh Day and the six days of Creation) . . .

That same binary system—those who follow and those who don't, those who are holy and those who are profane—showed up again in a magazine I used to pick up in the yeshiva's library, *Highlights for Children.* I found it fairly biblical in its judgments of two imaginary boys called Goofus and Gallant. (You could easily call them Cain and Abel, Isaac and Ishmael, Jacob and Esau.)

While Goofus would not say "please" or "thank you," Gallant would be very polite. Goofus, like Esau wolfing his mess of pottage, would reach across the table and grab. Gallant would say, "Would you please pass the sugar?"

I made up some of my own:

Goofus eats shrimp cocktail. Gallant says, "No, thank you, that's not exactly kosher."

Goofus worships idols (he bows to little plaster saints in his room). Gallant is faithful to a God who is everywhere, who has no form and requires the leap of imagination.

Goofus goes shopping on the Sabbath day. Gallant goes to services, then eats *cholent* (a heavy bean stew), naps, and later enjoys a leisurely *shaptzier* with his parents, greeting all the neighbors and sharing his accomplishments with them. He says "hello" politely to Mrs. Friedman.

Goofus likes to shoot birds with BB guns. Gallant is kind to the mother bird, and if he needs the eggs, he sends her away so she will not feel anguish. He will never eat a hunted animal—they must all be ritually slaughtered, with a blessing. Their blood, which is the soul, must not be tasted.

Goofus fails school and can never conjugate the Hebrew verbs. Gallant becomes a doctor—no, a specialist. In his spare time he reads the Talmud in the original Aramaic.

Goofus lives in Riverdale and doesn't know even which day is Sukkot. Gallant knows, and eats challah in the sukkah with his parents.

When I ask Rabbi Lichtiger about all these rigid judgments and separations I see in Judaism, he thinks about it for a minute, adjusts his black, silky yarmulka, and says.

"How wonderful that you ask, *maydeleh*. The meaning of the word *Israel* is *wrestles with God*. Do you remember how we read about Jacob wrestling with the angel?"

"Yes."

"That is what the greatest rabbis did. God loves questions."

Rabbi Lichtiger was a big door-opener in my life. All I had were questions. Some of them were my parents', but increasingly, more of them were mine.

Beauty Queen

To me, the most important holiday of all was the post-biblical one called Purim. There was once a king in Persia called Ahasuerus. He's kind of stupid, and kind of a drunk, but he's very powerful, and his kingdom is enormous. When his own wife does not obey him, he sends for all the beautiful women in the land, looking for a new bride. Amongst these women is Esther, who just happens to be secretly Jewish. Ahasuerus picks her to be his new queen.

Imagine that. *I* did.

"No, not the blonde. Not the redhead. That one with the light-blue eyes, nah. Wait, wait—I see someone I like! Look at that black hair! Those big dark eyes. And she seems to be quite intelligent, too!"

"Yes! I'll be very helpful to you! I get a lot of stars! Pick me!"

"I do—I pick *you!*"

Meanwhile, the king's advisor, Haman, decides that the Jews are bad and dangerous, and must be annihilated. They draw lots (*purim*), and choose the date for this genocide.

Esther, learning about this plan, bravely runs to the king. Esther knows that it is dangerous to enter the royal chambers unless Ahasuerus has allowed it by showing his golden staff, but she enters anyway.

She finds him in a loving mood.

"Why, Esther, my beauty, what is wrong?"

"What is wrong is that Jewish people are going to all be killed soon! And no one is going to stop it! God might be busy, you never know! Maybe *you* should do something!"

And he says, "But Esther, my love, why do *you* care?"

And she tells him, "I care because these are my people. I, the woman you love, am actually a Jew myself," she says, "a Jew like my mother's father, the one with the blonde moustache and cornflower-blue eyes."

The king does not dip her head in the trough over and over, nor send her or her relatives to their deaths in Dachau. Instead, he immediately saves the Jews and sends their enemy Haman to his death. Because of Esther, all the Jews in Persia are saved. Purim is celebrated on the day that the Jews were meant to be destroyed. It is a happy day of mischief and masquerade. Jews are even allowed, no, urged, to get drunk on that day.

At Yeshiva Soloveitchik, every girl dressed up as Esther on Purim. Since we were all fairly poor, we'd portray our beauty queen in our mother's lipstick. Bunny Milcher wore a hot magenta, like Jayne Mansfield. I wore Revlon's Cherries in the Snow, and was sure that I was transformed into an irresistible future queen when I rubbed it over my lips (perhaps a bit of tooth as well). Then we girls would add a bobbly beaded necklace (in the Wilma Flintstone vein) and a golden paper crown with square, plastic gems in it. Some preferred a woolen, paisley scarf slug over their hair like babushkas, tied under the chin. Bunny added sparkling white cat-eye sunglasses without the lenses, broken shades her mother had once worn in Miami. Glamorous.

The boys wore paper eye-masks, which, with their gold and purple swirls surrounding the eyeholes, were meant to evoke the exoticism of the famous king of Persia. Most also wore their clothes backward, a witty fillip to the art of masquerade. Buttons down the back of a boy's shirt or cardigan! Like a girl! You can just imagine the merriment.

One day, I mused, tar-head crushed under my cardboard crown, I too would capture the heart of a savior, my own potentate. I would make him love me and my people—and that is how our suffering would end. All I had to do was grow up and become beautiful. Which was not easy, because I was developing into quite a scrawny and pale girl, with thick glasses and buck teeth. When I'd keep asking my father if I was beautiful, he'd still answer, annoyingly, "There are more important things than beauty."

What, in heaven's name, what?

MY BROTHER'S BIRTH was a grand consolation to my mother and grandmother. Gita had lost not only a father but two teenage brothers, who had been shot by the Nazis while still in the Kovno ghetto. So this little boy, Manny, who bore her father's name (embodied in the first initial "M") and carried his faded memory in a boy's healthy body—what joy!

On the other hand, Manny tended to irritate my touchy, proud father. He was a spirited boy, full of humor, sass, and challenge. Nowadays, he might have been labeled "hyperactive" before he finished a single zigzagged lap around the block, but at that time, he was simply a typical, mischievous boy. My father, however, saw him through God's judgmental eyes. He had bought into Judaism's dualities—day and night, Jacob and Esau, right and wrong, us and them. My brother, to him, was "them."

Having known no father himself, he saw his boy as Esau: threatening, wild, and primitive. Dr. Benjamin Spock was on most night tables in those days, but not on my parents'.

Thus, unlike the indulgent and stage-sensitive developmental pediatrician, my father saw unique defiance in his son's every age-appropriate kick and raspberry. What was he to make of a little boy who seemed to learn about life from Dennis the Menace (a true paradigm of hyperactivity), Huck Finn, or Howdy Doody—who knew, and relished knowing, that he was "just a kid"?

"Hey! You're hurting me!" my brother would say. "And I'm just a kid!"

What did the phrase *just a kid* mean to someone like my father? He had never been "just a kid." After his father had been shot by the Cossacks, my father had had to be unwaveringly strong for his mother. There was no part of his life that had not witnessed tragedy and demanded sacrifice and resolve. So he had little experience with children, other than assuming that they obeyed their revered parents without question, as he had done.

My father could not afford books for school. An athletic, resourceful boy who ice-skated everywhere in his frozen Baltic village, he was often forced to lend his skates in order to borrow a book and try to catch up. Even with his two older siblings becoming independent, he saw that he was a drain on his mother. So by age thirteen, instead of preparing for a Bar Mitzvah, he settled down to the discipline and promise of hard work. Later, he enrolled in the Lithuanian army and thrived under the rigors that, he felt, made him equal to all other men, rich or poor, Jewish or not. He believed in sacrifice, in unwavering routines. He had loved the army, where, he often told me, the officers complimented him on his being a good soldier "for a Jew."

How equipped was he to deal with American children, nourished and spoiled and played with and idolized?

From the start, when my brother began to shout "No!"—
sometimes punctuating his resistance by jumping up and
down—my father took his little boy's bravado as another
mortal threat.

"WHAT did I hear?"

"You heared me say NO, Daddy!"

"YOU—DARE—say 'NO'—to ME???"

"Yes, Daddy," said my poor, normal, American brother,
a kid with whom any other less exhausted dad would have
loved to play catch.

"Yes Daddy what?"

"YES I Say NO to YOU!!"

A beating followed, and would follow for years (for
neither would stand down), ceasing only when my father's
arms were tired. This was a process called *shmitz* in Yiddish, a
cognate for the word *smite* (which the biblical God was often
wont to do). It was methodical, brutal, and sad.

Yiddish has several words for hitting. There is the *frask*—
a sort of slap (I received *frasks* from my mother for being
"fresh," but never on the face). There is a *klahp*—more of
a one-time blow. And then there is the far more serious
shmitz—implying a more sustained beating, perhaps with
a belt (the dreaded *rimmen*). My father had no need for
the weaponry of buckles. His own massive hands drove the
fierce message home.

"OW! HEY! STOP! OWWWWW!"

"Oy Shimon! Herr opp!" My mother would cry, which
would make my father even wilder. He hated tears; they
added to his rage.

"THIS! WILL! TEACH! YOU! TO ANSWER ME LIKE
THAT!!"

"Watch his head! Pass opp zein kopp!"

"AN! ANIMAL! YOU! HAVE! TO! BEAT!"

"Ushtaks, Shimon!" Now she spoke Lithuanian to him. Stop!
And then he would finally stop, exhausted.

With loud theatrical sobbing, my brother crumpled on
the linoleum.

"I think you broke my head, you baldy!"

"WHAT DID YOU CALL ME?"

"Nothing."

It was simply impossible for my poor father to be domi-
nated, or imagine the challenge of domination, by anyone,
of any size, anymore. And his son was made of the same determined cloth. As for me, I picked up right away that it was
best never to contradict my father. Not openly. I could never
decide if my brother was brave or stubborn for challenging
his unstoppable, windmill-fisted father.

My mother found my supposed immunity annoying.
"Why don't you ever hit *her*?" I once heard her say, after her
boy had been beaten down and quieted.

"Is she too special to hit, your precious Sonia?"

Progression in my mother's preference for my brother
(who, like her, suffered from her husband's wrath). Progression in her steadfast resistance to me and my supposed
charms. Here is my deepest loss, a life increasingly lacking
in my mother's good will, in which all my successes became
her failures, and fueled a subtle, seemingly perverse resistance to both my father and me. I seemed to represent a
challenge to her: all the books she did not read, all the insights she did not understand, all the messages to me that
my father never gave her.

"Let *her* be in the kitchen, *you* need to study," he'd say to
me, of my mother.

That was fine with me, but all my mother wanted was

a daughter with her in the kitchen, particularly when her mother died and left her alone. Liba had been hospitalized for pneumonia, caught, my mother said, when she'd picked me up from school on a wintry day. One night in the hospital, the nurse didn't come when Liba had rung for her. Needing to go to the bathroom, she had climbed out of her bed, over the iron railing, fallen, and broken her hip. Not long after, an embolism in her lung had killed her. My mother was left, as she saw it, alone. Her husband was no substitute for the mother she adored, her confidante, her best friend. And I, perhaps the cause of her greatest loss (she had saved her mother from the Nazis but not from me), was meager comfort.

When I played the piano, a flashy, precocious version of my mother's dimensional virtuosity, Simon had commented: "Gita, you play faster, maybe your pieces are a little harder. But Sonia, you put more feelings into your few notes than I have ever heard from your mother. You brought tears to my eyes." And this was no metaphor; he would actually wipe his eyes. It was really unfair—she was the one who had studied all her life, who, even now, enjoyed those lessons with Mrs. Ruskin. I didn't even really know my scales, and hated practicing.

Later, my mother would make sure she weighed in on the matter.

"Oh, you're so smart," she'd say by the time I was ten. "Such a talent. I really admire you." Young as I was, I was aware of the bitterness. It came from a side of her that hated to be shown up by another woman, and her daughter, at that. Though she loved me, I felt she truly did not like me. It frightened me that any strength I had seemed to weaken her. Even strengths that I really didn't have, like knowing who I was outside the world of praise.

My Helen Keller Fixation

ANOTHER RIFT between my mother and me arose be cause of the most famous blind and deaf person in the world. One Sunday, as she often did, my mother took my brother and me to the movies. Usually the films were light and fluffy Hollywood fare, but this time, as the lights went out, there was no Doris and no Rock. Instead, the screen illuminated in somber black and white and the words *THE MIRACLE WORKER.*

Suddenly, with no warning, I was lost in the world that came to life before me. Sitting in the darkness, I met the tragic child, cursed in her crib to be different. No one understood Helen Keller, no one knew her. Treated like an animal, in pain and wailing, lost in a world of unreferenced pain. Kicking. Trying to escape. Until the teacher came and released all her beauty. Until someone finally freed her from her jail.

When the lights rose, I could not move from my seat. My brother and my mother were already standing in the aisle, ready to move on and out to the delicatessen nearby. Then they noticed me, sitting in a daze. I begged my mother to stay and wait with me for the next showing. Sometimes, if a movie was really good, we did that. If I had had my way, I would have sat in that dark theater all day, waiting for the lights of the story to unfold, waiting for Helen's inner light to be revealed. But my mother had found the movie disturbing. Worse, still, was my reaction to it. She hated when I was intense like my father. She hated when I was weird and fixated and dramatic about something she could not or would not feel.

Even so, I could not shake the spell of *The Miracle Worker*; I took the movie home with me, and it went wherever I went.

"WATER!" I screamed, pouring showers from the faucets in the kitchen, in the bathroom, and running from one to the other, splashing my hands and face.

Not *vasser*, as in Yiddish. "Water."

"Bist du ganz meshugeh?" Are you completely crazy? What had she done to deserve a daughter like this?

"I'm Helen Keller!" I replied. I even loved the name. The pain of her private "hell" was embedded in the first name. *Keller* meant *cellar* in Yiddish and German. That is where her soul had been stuck, in fear and in hiding.

"God forbid you should be a Helen Keller!" my mother screamed.

From that day on, my mother forbade me from talking about my idol and multiply disabled doppelganger. She did not know, however, that my school had a Scholastic book on which the movie had been based. Helen herself (what a prodigy) had written her own memoir, which I took out of the library and renewed and renewed and renewed.

From her book, I learned that Helen Keller had, despite her misfortunes (or maybe because of them), resolved to go to Radcliffe, then the sister school to Harvard. This was what she deemed to be the hardest, toughest, and most demanding school in the world. Helen would prove herself. Just to show them. It was not enough for her to walk and talk and do everything "normal" people did. Normal was not part of the equation for Helen. She was no Bunny Milcher who went to Miami in the winter, whose mother wore magenta lipstick and blue mascara, who wanted to be "average and happy." She was great; she wanted to be abnormal and different and special. Like my father and maybe like me.

I also learned that Helen, having graduated from Radcliffe with honors, had gone on tours, speaking (in her way) to audiences worldwide. These audiences loved her inordinately. This woman was extraordinary. She had been deaf and blind and treated like an animal. But once released . . . so special. All they could do was wildly applaud.

And Helen Keller would say (this brought tears to my eyes):

"I can hear your applause through my feet."

Which only made them applaud all the more, and ecstatically stomp their feet to broaden her private smile.

My father let me talk to him about Helen Keller when my mother was not around. He was there when I had nightmares; he was the one who got up in the night. I had woken from one of my bad dreams about being asphyxiated (the tonsillectomy had led to years of such dread). As he sat by my side, Simon explained that the operation had not been a punishment, but a vital step in my ultimate betterment.

"It hurt for a while, yes, you had to suffer. But now you are no longer sick all winter. Your body is more strong."

"Yes," I said, "I understand. You have to have some bad thing happen for a good thing to happen."

"Like working hard for good grades," he offered. "The lazy one thinks he did enough, but the strong one studies all night, as I have seen you do. As the Torah says, 'Those who plant with tears shall reap with joy.'"

I thought this a good opportunity to turn the conversation over to my heroine, Helen Keller. "I actually have this theory," I said. "It's called 'God compensates and balances everything.'"

"Yes, good, tell me more," said my father, sounding like my teachers at school. My father knew what being "special" was; he knew that he himself was special, that despite all his troubles God always took extra care of him. At the eleventh hour, perhaps, but that was His way with the Jewish people, was it not?

"You know who Helen Keller is, Daddy?"

"The whole world knows this person," said my father. By that time, we subscribed to *Time* and *Life* and *Look* magazines. Even my father was beginning to know what most Americans knew about the people in the firmament of fame.

"Helen Keller got sick when she was little, you know, very sick, and no *spritz* could help, and then became blind and deaf. What could be worse?"

Before he could answer—for of course he'd have a ready, Holocaust-based answer to "What could be worse?" (for example: "It's worse to see your child shot before you and hear his cries!")—I said:

"But! On the other hand, God gave her all the brains, the soul, the charm, and the energy."

"Who—to Helen? You know what? I think He gave the same to you!"

Now he was talking.

"Thanks, Daddy. Do you really think so?"

"You know what I think. I think you are very, very special. Our Father in Heaven gave you so much."

"But I mean, about Helen Keller, that no matter how much trouble there is in your life, there is a wonderful, beautiful answer inside of you."

"They say that blind people's other senses get more sharp," he noted. He was also reading his *Reader's Digest*.

"So maybe sad people could get more, more deeply happy in their way, Daddy. They have the power to be as happy as they had been sad before, right?"

He understood what I meant. We both felt the depth that came from our tragic history, and the release, or relief, that survival implied.

"So when Helen Keller finished Radcliffe, it was better than anyone else finishing Radcliffe. Look how far she had come. She wasn't just some smart rich girl who had it made, whose mother and grandmother had studied there, or who had a rich American father."

"And so the world clapped for her more than anyone else,"

"Yes, they applauded her more than anyone else. So loud that, instead of just hearing it, she could FEEL it with her whole entire body."

Then my father wrapped me tight and warm in my blankets, and I fell into a safe and hopeful sleep.

Lucky Number 13

THE YEAR a child becomes a teenager is always going to be memorable, but this passage is indelibly marked on the mind of a Jewish child. My brother, at thirteen, was now considered a man according to the Jewish law. Tall and slim, Manny was now a magnet for the opposite sex. At his Bar Mitzvah, he stood smiling as the photographer lined up all the girls from his class, as well as the Riverdale girls, daughters of my parents' friends. They leaned toward him, swooning from the left and from the right, as my brother stood, cool as Hugh Hefner, at the center. During Passover, only a month earlier, I had been surprised by the radical changes in Manny. Our parents had taken us to a hotel for the seders for the first time, and I had looked forward to exploring the "game room" with him. I had heard all about pinball machines and couldn't wait to try one.

Imagine my shock to find my brother utterly uninterested in "hanging out" with me, and instead, calmly leaning against a wall as females surrounded him. My brother was holding court! I overheard him whisper something about his "kid sister," and felt nothing but shame and loss as a pretty girl with long hair giggled beside him. This night was, sadly, different from all the other nights before.

I was, at this time, at the peak of physical cluelessness. At the Bar Mitzvah, my mother and I wore matching yellow dresses. Gita, with her English-rose complexion and green eyes, looked lovely in a sleeveless lemon gown with a sequin bodice and swirling chiffon skirt. My own awkward variant on her dress, besides washing out my sallow complexion, featured a nincompoop's bow in the back, which I cunningly matched by clipping yellow velveteen bows into my teased (and optimistically "flipped") hair. When the friendly photographer asked me for "that million-dollar smile," unfortunately, I obeyed. Buckteeth, knock-knees, lacquered black pompadour and velveteen bow-clips—this is why that picture has been in storage for years. King Ahasuerus Beauty Contest–ready I was not.

Still, from this point, life became thrilling. That same year, we moved to a nicer apartment, in a better neighborhood within the Heights. Now, we lived right near Fort Tryon Park, from whose high promenades we could see the forest green Palisades across the Hudson. The buildings were bigger, cleaner, brighter; their bricks were red and white instead of brown; the glass on their doorways, Art Deco; the living rooms elegantly "sunken," with two steps and a wrought iron railing.

German Jews actually lived in my new building—quietly prosperous scions of families like Schiff and Warburg! You could walk right by the venerable Breuer's Yeshiva, stark and forbidding, to which the dignified Jews from Berlin and Vienna sent their children. On our Shabbat *shpatziers*, they would tip their hats to my father and mother. The bakeries up here carried Sacher torte and Linzer tarts, the "appetizing" stores featured the rarest Aufschnitt—cold cuts with peas, cold cuts with aspic gelée. Real German wurst (yet Glatt Kosher). Maybe we never moved to the suburbs and got the dog, but I was wildly happy to be part of this haute bourgeoisie.

Soon, too, I would leave Yeshiva Soloveitchik and transfer to a modern Jewish academy called the Ramaz School. I would take a bus that sped me out of Washington Heights, past Harlem, and onto the splendor of Fifth Avenue. And just before this transformation, as the ultimate celebration of my brother's Bar Mitzvah, my family took its first plane trip abroad. It took us almost a solid day as we stopped in London, Rome, and Athens, headed for the Promised Land!

Israel was a young country then, not much older than my gangly big brother. It stood on shaky colt's feet, and our joy in it was innocent. Everyone on the El Al plane sang newly minted Israeli songs, clapping their hands like schoolchildren. When we stepped out, we descended a ramp, blinking into God's white hot eyes, and then we kissed the dusty, precious ground. Every second was significant with millennia of meaning. My parents' eyes were as bright as children's, and I remember feeling a deep sense of relief.

Despite my enjoyment of school, by the age of ten I was feeling such an ineradicable, exhausting sadness that strangers would say, "Hey, are you okay?" I often, unwittingly, looked as though I were about to cry. My posture was increasingly slumped, and I sighed a lot. Six million Jews had died, and this knowledge increasingly weighed me down. Day and night, I thought of it; day and night, I wanted to figure out why it happened and what could be said or done to make things right again.

Here in Israel, I felt my burden lightening. Being here was healing; it was God gathering us together again, as He had always promised. It was a place for all the Jews who had had nowhere else to go. At that time, I believed that only by the prayers of six million sacrificed souls did God finally grant the wishes of his people and give them back their long-lost homeland. Their souls were now the wind at our back, our luck and our new future.

We traveled to my uncle Israel's house—that was his actual name. One of my mother's distant cousins, Israel had left Europe a decade before the Holocaust as a pioneer. He lived in Tel Aviv, then a sleepy metropolis where every few blocks you could buy fresh squeezed, slightly warm grapefruit juice—*mitz eshkoliot*. Here, people spoke Hebrew and Yiddish. And everybody looked like my father and mother—down to the socks with sandals and the straw hats that both my father and mother wore in the summer. His was a fedora (with a small feather); hers, a broad sunhat, dainty string tied under the chin. Aunt Ruchama looked like my mother—bright-cheeked and maternal in her cotton flower shift. Though a distant relative, and by marriage at that, she was the first "auntie" I'd ever known.

Shortly after our arrival, I developed a fever, and Ruchama offered to take care of me. As my parents and brother went off on their first day of touring, she settled me on the sofa with a pillow behind my head and another under my knees.

Uncle Israel and Auntie Ruchama lived on the ground floor of a simple, square, three-story building made of dusty white stones. Through open doors of green plastic I saw a cool veranda and heard the sweet sound of birds twittering. There were sprinkles of sand on the white paving stones; we were close to the Mediterranean. A little palm's leaves waved, and near it, a long table held an enormous watermelon. Ruchama noticed me gazing outdoors, and said:

"Now I am going to do something really special for you. I am going to make it cool and beautiful, like Gan Eden (the Garden of Eden)!

"Do you like Gan Eden?"

"Ken!" I responded in Hebrew. Yes!

She put one slow fan on my right, and one on my left. The air was fragrant with flowers and salt water.

Then she went to the veranda and brought in the watermelon, which she called *avati'ach*. She ran into the kitchen, and a few minutes later ran back with a plate full of watermelon slices.

"They look like smiles, Auntie," I said.

"Of course, they are smiles, *motek sheli*," she answered. My sweetness.

The next day, Ruchama announced: "Now, you are going to have a real treat. Ice caffe!"

Disappearing again into the kitchen, she emerged with a tall glass filled with coffee, ice, and vanilla ice-cream.

"It's good, no?"

"Metzuyan!" Excellent.

These two words, "yes," "excellent," were the first I spoke in this ancient language in the place where it had first originated. Israel was only a teenager, not much older than my brother and I. Everyone spoke this biblical tongue in everyday life, no matter where they had come from. It was a Babel in reverse, language embraced as a form of salvation.

Coming back from his first tours of the Promised Land,

my father beamed with pride. "I have never felt so good," he said simply. "Everyone here is a Jew like me, even the policeman and the farmer!"

Much of Israel had long lain fallow, arid and dusty, and where it had not been dusty, it had been ridden with malarial swamps. In Jerusalem, ancient Hebrew graves had been trampled, holy places defiled. (We still could not go to the Western Wall of the Temple; it was not open to Jews.) It had been like a spurned bride. And now, as the prophets had promised, it had been loved, and tilled, and prayed over, and danced upon to the sound of tambourines. Once again, it was green and fruitful, and flowing with milk and honey.

This hopeless wilderness, from which we had been banished for nearly two thousand years, soon led the world in its production of citrus fruits, of flowers! Kibbutzim were full of orange groves, and people from all over the world came to help us pick them. The soldiers of the Israel Defense Forces—imagine, a Jew able to defend himself—were young and strong, tall and olive-skinned, macho and handsome. Even the girls seemed to have muscles and military postures, though their eyes were full of life and mischief.

I could see this for myself. My uncle drove us around in his Deux Chevaux, wearing the short-sleeved shirt every Israeli man wore, even the president. Elbow hanging out the car window, suntanned and casual, he honked his horn indiscriminately to move the sluggish traffic, or to say hello to someone he knew. Everyone knew one another. It was a big Jewish party, a party of survivors.

I thought of the pilgrimage holidays we learned about in school—Pesach, Shavuot, and Sukkot. How thousands had once thronged together, bearing harvests, goats bleating (like the cars did now)—and how it must have felt to live as a Jew in those days. I was Eve, thinking of Eden—and I was in Eden. In yeshiva, we used to recite the old verse: "If I forget thee, O Jerusalem, let me forget my own right arm." Every Passover, we prayed (as did generations before us): "Next Year in Jerusalem!" And now we were here.

I looked at the arms of many of the Jews here. Working, driving the bus, handing me an ice cream or falafel in pita, so many of these working arms were covered with tattoos from Europe, numbering them for a mass grave. How amazing that they had managed to escape to this land of sunshine, watermelon smiles, and ice caffe. My parents' nightmare was over, I hoped; all would be good from now on.

A Small Celebrity

IN A JERUSALEM PARK, an incredible thing happens. My father and I enter the cool green groves, full of royal palm trees, tropical bushes, and waves of pink-red bougainvillea. My mother and brother, just behind us, are buying fresh, foaming grapefruit juice from a street vendor at the entrance. My father is dressed like a free man on vacation—in a patterned short-sleeved shirt and belted, beige Bermuda shorts. Before Israel, I had never seen him step outside without a suit and tie. I, too, am wearing shorts, yellow, with a lime-green shirt and summery white sandals. Wiggling my toes in the soft air, I exhale with happiness and a sense of relief. Everyone is relaxed in my family. Time stands still amid the noble palm trees and kind, soft flowers. Time hovers here like hummingbirds, like whirring watch-works, so fast as to seem motionless.

People stroll past us. And then a couple stop in their tracks—a man dressed casually like my father, a woman in a flowered blouse and turquoise skirt. Nothing special—here, everyone looks like my parents. But they have stopped, and the man is staring at us.

"Simon! Simon Taitz?"

My father looks at him. The stranger's eyes slowly fill with light, as though he has seen an angel from heaven.

Two more men rush over, one with a beautiful Saint Bernard on a leash, the other clutching a small boy in each hand.

"What did you say? Is it him?"

"Can it be?"

"Taitz-the-Watchmaker?" one says, as though that is the essence of who my father is.

Men, women, children. All venture forth to surround him, touching his arm, hugging his neck. He is perplexed— why are they all around him, especially? Do they all know one another? Simon Taitz at last begins to soften, to smile; he laughs, confused and expectant. Israel is a place where Jews like him, whom nobody wanted, can be loved.

More dogs come to him, pulling their owners and wagging their tails, joining in the fuss over the new celebrity. My father pats their heads, and a docile German shepherd licks his hand. He looks like a king, a good one, back from exile and receiving tribute. And then I hear the words that explain everything.

"This man saved us!" shouts one. "Zeh ha-ish shehitzil otanu!!"

"You hear that, Dovid? Yosef?" says the man with the two little boys. "This man saved *Abba* in the camps!"

"I was in your workshop in the war, Mr. Taitz!"

"In Dachau!" says another. "You saved us!"

"Because of you we are alive!"

An older man in a sky blue shirt that matches his eyes bends over to whisper a secret in my ear:

"Your father is a great, great man."

"I always knew it," I say.

That day, I learn that my father rescued many people in the war, in his watchmaker's workshop at the Dachau concentration camp. Like a Jewish Oskar Schindler, he had gathered one man after another into the safety of his shelter, teaching them how to lean over a workbench, loupes in their eyes, tools in their hands, and act as though they were fixing watches. He himself did the technical work, and meanwhile, the other men within the growing workshop stayed indoors during the harsh winters. He regularly asked for more food for them, and they were fed. The Nazis, he had always told me, loved punctuality.

"In a way," he always said, "they respected me and my work."

Simon had marked the hours, minutes, and seconds of his own nightmare. He sensed that he would survive, that he had a mission to live and tell.

Now I know why my father felt so close to God. They were helping each other, here on earth. Perhaps being Jewish did put one in an uncomfortable position, but it was also a front-row seat to history, and here and there one could be a hero—a real one, a savior, the chosen of chosen.

And that is why on that long-ago day, there were hugs and tears of joy, redemption and hope, in the heart of Jerusalem, the broken but still beating heart of the world.

I AM IN LOVE WITH ISRAEL and the idea of the Jewish hero (and heroine). Through word of mouth, my parents hear about a summer camp that follows the spirit of early Zionism. In that time, over a century ago, Israel had been a dream, and an Austrian Jew, Theodor Herzl, was mocked for saying, "If you want it, it is no legend." It turned out that Herzl, who became the father of Zionism, was right. This camp, Betar, is dedicated to the spirit of its first pioneers, who wanted nothing more than a homeland of their own. The summer after our trip to Israel, my parents send me there for eight weeks.

I am eleven years old, and have never been away from my parents, but yeshiva has drilled the soul of the biblical prophets into mine. I know that my father is a hero in a broken world. The chants and songs of this intense place rouse and mesmerize me. Like a drumbeat, they stir my impressionable blood with thoughts of ultimate redemption.

"Do you want to go to Israel? Do you want to go on *Ali-*

yah, to rise up and be free in your own land?" we are asked, but only rhetorically.

"Yes! I've been there!" I pipe up. "I wanna go back!"

Most of the knock-kneed girls around me, kicking up dirt on the weedy grounds, could not care less about Jewish history or Israel. Tough girls from the Bronx, Brooklyn, and Long Island, they "make out" and "get felt up" by boys in the bushes; they pierce each other's ears with sewing needles. I wonder if everyone has been sent to this camp by accident— ads in the papers were ubiquitous, and the fees, I later learn, ridiculously low. Here's why: there are no normal camp activities. There is a small, scummy lake whose entry-level mud sucks like quicksand, horrible barrack-like bunks, and, for sports, tetherball and potato-sack races. For me, however, this place is no accident, but a perceived form of destiny. For those who are interested in more than simple summer fun, the camp provides a special path.

I soon decide that I want to be a Betari, an elite group within Camp Betar that adheres to a radical form of Jewish nationalism. To become part of this club, you have to learn Jewish military history and vow to "fight for freedom"—even to the point of death.

I want to be a Betari
I want to set my country free!

We stand together in the "uniform" of white shirt, navy shorts, and neckerchief. My hair, finally longer, is up in a high, tight ponytail; many of the older girls have long, thick braids that seem to mean serious business. My sneakers happen to be weird: my mother, who shops for me at her beloved John's Bargain Store, where most shoes are sold from a large table, has found the world's first pair of pointy sneakers. These points have never been in style, and perhaps will never be. But in this group, no one notices or cares.

We sing together, and when we say "my country" we mean Israel. Yes, it is technically "free"—between horrors for the moment—but we are obsessed by its history of fragility. This continuous looking-backward to the point of greatest trauma is familiar to me. Most of the other Betaris—like elite Scout members—are older than I am. Some have patrolled in neighborhoods where Jews are teased or ambushed. But I have been in military training of sorts for a long time myself.

We stand on the grass in front of our bunks and shout: *Tel Chai!* The hill lives! The hill is a hill in Judea that was conquered almost 1,000 years ago. This yeshiva girl, whose soul was swept up in millennial sources from birth, is having a heyday. Betar lives in the past. Even though the strongholds of Yodephet, Masada, and Betar have long fallen to ancient Rome (itself long gone), we swear that they will never, ever, be conquered again.

In order to assure this, we are given old .22 caliber rifles for target shooting, and are taught the rudiments of judo. Throwing a group leader across my hip, I imagine throwing "the enemy" as he jumps me. Thump! On the mat you go, and stay there! We hear of saboteurs who crawled through the nettles to kill settlers in the first Israeli kibbutzim. Enemies in the night, throat-cutters. What kind of people would kill Holocaust survivors?

There is a song we sing on Passover:

Ela shebechol dor vador
Omdim aleinu lechalotaynu.

In every generation, they stand up and try to finish us. But, the song continues:

Vehakodosh Baruch Hu
Matzilaynu miyadam
And the Holy Blessed God saves us from their hands.

After the Holocaust, we had begun to question God's timing. Okay, he "saved" us, you could say, but it *was* certainly a case of too little, too late. So maybe it would be a good thing if, for once, we could save ourselves. As the rabbis teach: "If someone comes to kill you, get up earlier and kill him." At Camp Betar, the primary Jewish ethos is survival. And it rests more in revivalist Zionism, in sheer practicality, in defending a land and freedom no one may take away from you, than in religion.

We will help out, we Betaris, named for a hill that, like the more famous Masada, fell to the Romans after a prolonged resistance, in the first century. The warriors of Masada choose to commit suicide rather than surrender, and we would eagerly do the same. Our camp is dedicated to the memory and philosophy of the early Zionist Josef Trumpeldor, who fought against British occupation. Plays are not put on about the Queen Esther who seduced a powerful king, but about brave Hannah Senesh, a young partisan girl who parachuted back into Europe in the middle of World War II and was executed. We all want to be like Hannah Senesh, who had immigrated to Israel to work the land, returning to Hungary only to help her people during the Nazi era. We all want to strap on a parachute and be let out in the right place, or the wrong place that needs to be set right. We can't wait.

We have learned that our enemies respect only one

thing—strength. So I stand straight and tall as a leader in khaki uniform, kerchief at his neck, shouts:

BETARIM, HIPAKED!
(MEMBERS OF BETAR, ATTENTION!)
Then,
HEYEH MUCHAN!
(BE READY!!)
To which we reply:
TAMID MUCHAN!!
(ALWAYS READY!!)

Is this the moment I have been waiting for? The one in which I get to DO SOMETHING to save my family, my people, my poor, persecuted fellow Jews? I am thrilled by the .22 caliber rifle, thrilled to be talking in Hebrew about "destiny," even though all I do is shoot blindly at bull's-eyes on old burlap. This is no normal Jewish camp, where you play badminton outside and jacks inside the bunk. This is a post-Holocaust camp, and it fits into my brain like a bracing antidote to sorrow.

We learn that anti-Semitism comes in many forms, and that it never goes away. That it is a devious and permanent sickness, born of envy and ignorance. Yes, the post-Holocaust world sent it underground, but it pops up again and again. This time, we will be ready. I, Sonia Taitz, with legs like spaghetti al dente, will be ready.

My mother is, of course, sane and skeptical.

"Yeah, yeah, you will be some great help. Meanwhile, you should learn first to make a good borscht." She wasn't being sarcastic in this instance. She really did, still, want me to learn to make a good borscht. Or anything remotely edible.

Redemption Song

THE SCHOOL I attend after the old yeshiva is a more modern Jewish preparatory academy on the posh Upper East Side of Manhattan. Its mission is to prepare Jewish children not only to follow the traditions, but also to get into Yale and Harvard. The change of schools, vast in measures of prestige, is my father's idea. It is also another giant step away from Washington Heights and my mother.

It is amazing that one long bus ride, on the #4, takes me from my parents' humble home, and then—as though breaking through storm clouds into the sun—to Fifth Avenue and the Museum Mile. Embassies, limestone mansions, millionaires.

As always, I am something of an outsider, a Jew among Jews. If, in Washington Heights, the elites were German Jews, here, on the Upper East Side, my classmates have apartments near Gracie Mansion with Japanese futons and Chinese triptychs, mothers who are slim and tall and wear elegant chignons, fathers who are lawyers and play golf. They have maids who live in "maids' rooms" in vast, high-ceilinged apartments, where the carpets are not wall-to-wall but Persian, afloat on a sea of polished parquet. These people are even more elegant than my parents' Riverdale crowd, who still have unsheddable accents along with their aspirations (they call their cars "Kedilecks").

I am most comfortable with short little Sarah, a scholarship girl, who always wears purple, whose hair is like Brillo, whose father is a diamond-cutter, who lives in the Bronx. Her parents speak Yiddish with a Polish accent, and her Bubbe lives downstairs. Whenever we are on the phone (most every night), I can hear a subway train pass by, which she tells me rattles her floor. I love Sarah. She is my only friend in the school with immigrant parents who worry and sigh. Even though the school shows horrible films each year on Holocaust Remembrance Day, bringing us all into an air-conditioned social hall to view Jewish bodies shoveled up by bulldozers and hauled into pits, and even though many of the girls' faces seem wet when the lights go up, Sarah really knows how to suffer, right now, here in America. When I talk about my pointy sneakers from John's Bargain Store, or a mother who never stops talking about her dead father and brothers, Sarah knows exactly what I mean. She shops at Loehmann's when she is lucky. All the other girls in this new school shop at Saks and at Bloomingdale's. They whip out credit cards with authority.

For the first time I realize that I am a minority in a minority, and that not all Jews are plagued by endless fears and mourning. Not a single one of the kids in my grade has even heard of Camp Betar. When I describe it, they wonder if I am really as "cool" as I pretend to be. (I am far too intense.) They go to "regular" Jewish camps, with tennis lessons, softball diamonds, and Olympic-size pools. Their homes are not little slummy apartments, and I don't invite them to mine.

Yes, we have moved up in the world—not to that promised house where I would have a dog like Thunder the Alsatian, and still in Washington Heights—but a step up nonetheless. The new apartment is on a street called Overlook Terrace, a name that evokes breezes and luxury, and real terraces, outdoor spaces where we can sit! (We no longer need to put folding chairs out on the street to catch a breeze.) Though our balcony is but a small rectangle hanging off the side of our building's façade, I feel as though we have a backyard, chaises, and even the possibility of a lawn. I buy some African violets and set them out to breathe the fresh air with me. "Oy, a mechayeh," as my mother would say, sitting there and taking a glass of cool water. Oh, this makes me live.

She loves the apartment, loves that it is a new construction, with air and light and marble in the lobby. She loves coming home every day, enjoying the cool when it is warm outside, the warm when it is cool outside, loving the kitchen, which is the center of the apartment, and not simply one more room along a narrow, dismal hallway.

The building also has an enormous outdoor pool, making me feel as though I have actually surpassed the suburbs and gone all the way to Beverly Hills. The entire development is new and modern (we are among the first tenants), which to us, at that time, means all things good. My mother is overjoyed that our bathroom is tiled in baby blue, that the entry to our apartment contains a small foyer featuring a closet with doors that slide on rollers, and that the doorbell no longer goes "*eeeeeccccchhhhhhhh*" but "*ding dong,*" like the Avon lady in the TV commercials.

But it's still not good enough for my new friends.

One problem is that my brother, ever taller and more

gangly, no longer has his own room. There are only two bedrooms—one for my parents, and a smaller one for me. Manny sleeps in the living room, on a "love seat" that turns into a bed. He has agreed to this arrangement because of the pool, and the pretty neighborhood, which is set on a hill. We live only a step, now, from the sanctuary of the vast and leafy Fort Tryon Park. From our perspective, it is like a secret forest. Though my parents and I tend to stick to the flower paths and the promenade overlooking the Hudson, parts of the park wind into subtle dead ends; there are granite rocks to climb and dark corners to discover. Manny is often there, exploring fun, teenaged things that my mother only hints about. He has left Yeshiva Soloveitchik, too, and is now enrolled in an elite public high school.

"Don't look in his pockets!" she warns me.

"What's in there?"

"Funny balloons!"

She doesn't say a word to him about the balloons. He is always her favorite and can do no wrong. His frequent prowling outdoors seems to her a healthy sign of manliness. When he returns, smelling of sweet, smoky perfumes and sporting strange marks on his neck, my mother offers him platters of food, ushering him to a chair in the kitchen as though he is a weary prizefighter between rounds.

Gita decorates her new home in glamorous shades of white and gold. The fiberglass curtains are heavy and white, with Greek-key patterns in gold. Gold, indeed, is a motif: Manny's convertible "love seat" is covered in gold silk, the carpet is thick and gold, and the pride of the room, a huge sofa, is white, with curved wooden arms and thick gold threads woven throughout. My mother loves this piece so much she covers it in customized plastic, complete with zippers. On top of it, she places square gold pillows, each with a button in the middle.

Still, even on Overlook Terrace, with its terraces and pool, even when my own new bedroom is furnished in brand-new white-and-gold French Provincial, even though it is now wallpapered with pink roses like some bedroom in Riverdale or even France, I am ashamed of where I live. Personally, I find it all beautiful and elegant. But my sophisticated new friends would not think so. They would ask, surely, "Where's your brother's room?" Each of them has a room of her own (even the maid). No one sleeps in the living room, where you can see them when you open up the front door.

And what am I to say? My hulking, hormonal teenaged brother sleeps on a fold-out bed; you can find it perpendicular to the sofa with the plastic covers on it?

What's more, Manny has turned into a hippie. His hair is thick, long, and wild; under his nose is a trace of a Fu Manchu; and his music is sepulchral and threatening. Unfortunately for me, there is a stereo in the living room, which my parents have bought so they can play songs from the *Fiddler on the Roof* cast album, or the *Reader's Digest Collection of Opera Greats*. But as they are always working, they rarely use the machine, which is housed in an enormous wall unit. Manny uses it.

My brother has awakened to the world of rock and roll. On his return from mystery excursions, he plays groups with odd names like the Troggs, the Fugs, the Animals, and Sam the Sham and the Pharoahs. Some of the lyrics, blasted into my ears, are disturbing:

Mother?
Yes, son?

I want to—(followed by a cacophonous drum solo suggesting unspeakable plunder)

This modern apartment's walls are thin, and the Fugs and Troggs invade my French Provincial, flower-papered sanctuary. My bedroom actually has *two* doors, halving my chances of privacy. Due to the advances of New World modernity, they are hollow, anything but soundproof. One connects me to my big brother's living room lair, the other to the kitchen, where my mother is likely to be banging pots, or making food my fancy new friends never heard of, like *klops.*

Despite this predicament, I gear up the nerve and ask one of the sweetest girls in the class to come over on a Sunday. She hesitates, then confides:

"My parents won't allow me to go to your house. They say it's in a bad neighborhood."

A bad neighborhood? 100 Overlook *Terrace?* Compared to 643 West 172nd Street, it is the Taj Mahal! But I have to acknowledge the fact that, as the years pass, crime is escalating, here as in the rest of the city. In our case, just south of us, and traveling north, is a busy drug trade, headed by new gangs of immigrants from Central America. Just a few blocks away, people have been thrown on the ground and mugged. We hear of shootings on the Channel Five 10 O'clock News. Car alarms blare at night. Sometimes, during our Sabbath strolls to the park, we are assaulted by booming music as convertibles screech by, triumphantly red with passion and heat.

So I travel to my friend's houses on East End and York Avenues, to Central Park West and Riverside Drive, and we stroll around the parks, dodging perverts, graffiti sprayers, butt pinchers, and marijuana smokers.

Most Jews, I learn, do not think about disasters every day! Their parents do not worry about saving money on clothes, or have accents that hint of their refugee status. They do not tell their children that the apple peels they don't eat could have saved lives in concentration camps. My classmates did not learn to shoot rifles at age eleven to save their hypothetical kibbutz from night-pillagers. They do not dream about shouting "tamid muchan!" when the world's alarm clock starts ringing. And they do not lie half awake every night, knowing that that alarm will soon ring.

Ever adaptable, I begin to relax, and even to luxuriate. Park Avenue is not having any Holocausts. The world, moreover, is loosening up in thrilling ways. Jews are increasingly acceptable, marriageable. The love-goddess, Marilyn, falls for the smart guy, Miller, with the glasses. Bushy-haired, big-nosed Bob Dylan steps onto the scene, and he's cool! He is followed by Barbra Streisand and Dustin Hoffman, who with those names and faces win big-screen love and Academy Awards. My friends and I chat about television shows, joking about the Judeo-quotient of favorites like *Bonanza* and *Mission Impossible*, Agent Maxwell Smart and his Agent 99, mod Peggy Lipton and Linda McCartney, née Eastman.

When I turn thirteen, there is no official Bat Mitzvah rite of passage; girls do not "go up to the Torah" in Orthodox circles, however modern or sophisticated. This silencing does not faze me, however. The outside world, to which I become more and more attuned, opens up in generous sync with my own adolescent blossoming. All is changing, we can see, morphing like the liquid in our lava lamps, turning old vendettas into an era of generous freedom. Being a woman, like being a Jew, becomes cool. In hip San Francisco, it's the Summer of Love; in England a waif called Twiggy evokes the dawn of the ambisexual; and in New York we caper around in miniskirts and hopeful white go-go boots. Half hysterical with excitement, I run to my friends' houses and dance to the hurdy-gurdy, higgledy-piggledy Beatles of *Sgt. Pepper's*. Rock and roll pounds the drumbeat of new and better times. I begin to understand my brother's newfound joie de vivre.

Enough with the worldwide conflicts and killings. We, the youth, boys with long hair and girls in pixie cuts, would make a new world. We were "the young generation," as the Monkees sang. The past was gone, for the first time, in our time. It was dead and daisied over. It was time to emerge from the bomb shelters, time for blossoms to poke out of gun barrels, .22 or otherwise.

This made sense to me, if not to my parents, who were wary of utopian fantasies. As a newly omniscient teen, I realized how sadly "blind" my parents were to my new world. All the "bad things," after all, had happened in Europe, that bloody old world of petty clanship. That is why everyone from there (except for the rockers) wore sour expressions and tweedy old suits and stockings and clunky high heels, while we could wear sandals and chain-belts and let our hair blow in the wind.

I remember my first makeup, all Brand X and yet more precious to me than Coty or Helena Rubinstein. Manny is thriving at his competitive high school; he is fencing and dating and busier than ever. But on a rare day when he has time, he takes me on an expedition to Woolworth's, within which I change my life. With his encouragement and support, I pick up a lipstick at this magical "five-and-ten-cent store." Its barrel is shiny gold; the color, Frosted Cocoa-Mocha, a crazy, mod bronze-beige. It smells of peppermint and feminine possibility. Then, the "blush on"—a cheap, plastic box with a clear rectangle revealing peachy powder, and a luxurious brush that turns the crumbling talc into a febrile glow on my cheeks. Later, in the bathroom, I rim my eyes with a black "kohl" pencil, imagining myself to be Nefertiti (if she'd worn peachy blush and frosted lipstick). Instantly, I am transformed from twit into temptress; if I could have looked at my face in the mirror all day (with some sort of gizmo attached to my head), I would have.

I throw my dumb stretchy hair bands away and learn to flip my hair by throwing it all forward and then letting it fall back in splendid leonine volume. Nature herself seems to be loving me, and I celebrate by wearing an assortment of boldly colored fishnet stockings to go with my go-go boots.

My parents scarcely notice these changes; during my teens they begin to enjoy a boom in their business and are now working harder than ever. In any case, I know enough to wipe off my makeup before entering the house. My father had commented, here and there, about the "paint" with which most American women were "shmeared": "In Europe, only prostitutes painted themselves like that; *Feh!*"

Now when I ask him, as I often have before, if I am beautiful, he does not tell me that beauty does not matter. He does not tell me that there are many other values in the world that go deeper and last longer. He looks at me, smiles, and says, with tremendous reverence:

"And now God has given you even that."

He makes me feel that my looks are a gift, but also a part of my arsenal, to be used when a life-or-death matter occurs, as it did to Scheherazade. Should my brains and stories not be enough, there can be my beauty. And vice versa. And should both fail, there is always the piano playing or recitation of Hebrew psalms in the original.

My mother, who wore only her bright swipe of Revlon Cherries in the Snow lipstick (with a pat of powder and clear nail polish on special occasions), seems unsure of what to say to her budding daughter in temptress regalia. The part of her that prefers Doris to Elizabeth might favor a less sultry look for her child, and yet she is gracious as I begin to transform.

"You have a classic beauty and a delicious *chen*," she says, using the Yiddish word for charisma. "The boys are going to love you," she continues, with the first trace of respect she has ever given me. It is a woman-to-woman comment, and it does me good. When one of my high school crushes comes running up the hill to Overlook Terrace, passing my mother walking down to the subway, she reports:

"You should have seen him run. Why did he run? Why do men run? I don't know. Maybe they run up the hill for you."

I was proud of this power. Love was always good, but in that era it seemed—as I'd always dreamed—to have revolutionary, matrix-altering potential. One was free to love anyone, be loved by anyone. Sexuality began to come out of hiding, and boundaries blurred. Nations blended, Afros were in, as were my friend Sarah's tight curls and my own shiny ultra-black hair. My heart swelled with hope. If there's only one life, let me live it as a sultry Schwarzkopf. Let me live, and not be pushed into the death-line because I might look a little "ethnic." Let me be saved, and hugged, and even loved.

Then came Israel's Six-Day War. Despite all this Haight-Ashbury, Electric Circus consciousness, I did not question

Israel's lightning-swift use of its forces to protect itself. Even in my dolly bird incarnation, a part of me was still that no-nonsense Camp Betar cadet and a war hero's daughter. When it came to my people, when it came to a threat of annihilation, I wanted a fighting chance.

Golda Meir, Israel's national grandma, said it well: "I can forgive my enemies for killing our sons, but I cannot forgive them for forcing us to kill theirs." I found her smart, strong, and oddly familiar, with the kind of orthopedic shoes my Bubbe wore. I felt safe with a prime minister like Golda at Israel's helm. Israel's face was female, with a corona of frizzy gray hair. Its founder, David Ben-Gurion, had his own Einsteinian coiffure. I loved this iconic grandpa for his casualness—he wore no ties; he was ready to push up his sleeves and plant a baby pine tree in the desert. Both he and Golda had new, Israeli, last names. "Meir" means "illuminating"; "Gurion" means "lion cub."

After six days, endlessly compared at my school to the miracle days of creation in Genesis, the Western Wall was ours to visit again, site of all those pilgrimages and millennial prayers. Although it was not even part of the Temple itself, just a wall outside it, photos showed soldiers, heads leaning against this powerful wall, helmets off, crying. Some became believers for the first time in their lives. All our learning had been a preface, like a prophecy from Isaiah— God will punish his people, but then God will redeem them.

"Ahavtich"—*I have always loved you*, the word I had learned in my old yeshiva. These were the forgiving times, the transcendent rapprochement I'd awaited all my life. I was glad my parents had lived to see not only Israel born, but its very heart restored, like an old pocket watch set ticking again.

Here was an answer to the awful documentary footage

Jewish schools showed each year on Holocaust Remembrance Day, piles of bodies scooped onto flatbed trucks or
dropped into ditches. Each time the camera closed up on a
face it looked like mine, or like the faces of my classmates,
or their families, or mine. And some of them must have
been their families, and mine.

We all want and need a happy ending, the comfort of,
if nothing else, a wall of stone. Stone to mark that we had
existed, the kind that Jews lay on graves to show they have
been there, that a life and a soul is acknowledged. Every Jew
on earth was not only a patriot that year, but a believer in
miracles on this earth, in our time.

The Making of a Courtesan

A T FOURTEEN, a great miracle happened there, as we say on Chanukah. Not, in this case, in the city of Modi'in, where Maccabee warriors battled Hellenized Syrians, but in my own developing body. Somehow, *finally*, I made the full transition from studious girl with coke-bottle glasses and braces to a sultry, Semitic Lolita with contacts, straight teeth, and killer curves à la Marilyn Monroe and Sophia Loren.

Still a child inside the modest Orthodox world, I did not know the true meaning of what I radiated for several more years. The first sign of this transformation was my English teacher, Mr. Levin, who suddenly said:

"And what is your opinion of this play, Sonia—you, you COURTESAN?"

This shouted, untoward word froze in the air. The moment passed. I suppose that none of us had the vaguest idea what a courtesan was, and Mr. Levin, always a bit fanciful, did have a tendency to shout out various wacky epithets. (I remember that he called one classmate "an ugly bowling ball." What did *that* mean?) When I hear the word now, I am almost flattered—for wasn't that what I had always dreamed about being—a modern Scheherezade-Esther? Yes, a courtesan—one who can make powerful men weak and susceptible.

Something beside my own subconscious intentions had brought out this reaction. One of the meaner boys had started sneezing every time I walked by, saying "Ah-choo! I'm allergic to foam rubber!" This was hilarious to him; "falsies" were apparently made out of foam rubber, and my breasts were big enough to seem improbable.

It was also of considerable advantage to me that my formerly despised, dangerous black hair was now considered sexy. I wore it straight, long, and glossy, an effect achieved by "wrapping" the hair around an empty coffee can. My looks were a political statement. Jews could be sexy, as were Italians and Puerto Ricans. I was an Indian Princess, or maybe even a Jewish American one. Nothing to be ashamed of. Ali McGraw played one in *Goodbye Columbus*, and the Holocaust wasn't mentioned even once. Finally, Jewish daughters could be spoiled, like Kitten in *Father Knows Best*. And when they grew up, these kittens could wrap men around their little fingers.

So *this* was how Helen of Troy addled Paris, how Cleopatra made Antony irrational. These clever women were blessed with brains, but to that were added more mysterious powers. The powers of the courtesan, the seductress, the femme fatale. My first perfume, after a brief false start with a girlish lily-of-the-valley, was called Tigress. It was musky, and the top of the bottle was covered in fake tiger fur. You can't get sexier than that, can you?

In my idiotic solipsism, in my vanity and adolescent fancy, I thought I had figured out some great abiding truth of the universe. Something that would solve all ethnic hatred, solve it in the simple union of man and woman whose love was so powerful that swords would be bent into wedding rings. The trouble with the Jewish people, over the years, and all the persecutions? That was simply because no sexy woman with a great big brain (and working knowledge of Rashi) had tried to *patiently explain* all the issues and unfairnesses. She had not yet had proper access to the right, all-powerful leader, the Billy Alpha Male, and no gentile man, busy riding horses bareback and generally being Nietzchean, had ever dreamed how wonderful love could really be.

If Hitler had met me, I thought, I could have had a few words with him, tossed my Tigress-scented hair, and averted all this nonsense. Okay, I would have dyed my Tigress-scented hair blonde. I wasn't stupid. I was, after all, a courtesan. Mata Hari must take many disguises. It is part of her dangerous yet thrilling mission to alter history. She does what she was born to do. Like Hannah Senesh, she dons her parachute and jumps, deliberately, into hostile land.

Despite my nascent female powers, I did not embark on a blissful ride on the highway of love. At first, it seemed easy. In my seventeenth summer, I met an appropriate male counterpart, a cute Jewish boyfriend. Yeshiva-bred like me, he was on the same summer tour of Europe for modern-Orthodox high school graduates. Jacob, like the other boys, wore a small woven yarmulka, and one day, as he and I were walking in Paris hand in hand, an old man had followed us. We wondered if he was one of the legendary European anti-Semites we had always heard about, and thought he would make some ugly comment about Jacob's religious headgear, or maybe mock our innocent young romance. As we walked more quickly, he pleaded, "S'il vous plait, mes enfants."

We stopped and turned around. The man was white-haired, tall and thin. He looked into our faces, tears in his warm brown eyes, and said, "Yiddishe Kinderlach . . ." Jewish children. "Yiddishe"—my maternal grandfather's word as the Nazis had taunted him. I patted the old man on the shoulder, and Jacob shook his hand. We were happy to be "Yiddishe Kinder" together, in Paris, representing the young, strong incarnation of our people.

In the fall, Jacob and I were both headed toward the same place—Columbia University in Morningside Heights—he to Columbia College, and I to Barnard, its female counterpart. We took turns sitting on Alma Mater's great, capacious, stone lap; we were thrilled to be received by the daunting, stern-hearted Ivy League. Tall and handsome, with shaggy brown hair and blue-green eyes, Jacob took care of me for nearly four years, waiting for me after classes, bringing me Drake's coffee cakes in the mornings, cooking small steaks for me on his little dorm toaster-grill.

Trust was there, and love followed over the next years. Jacob was my first partner, and I his. I loved being in his tiny room in John Jay Hall, entwined with this sweet man, laughing. We were compatible; we were like twins. In every picture taken of us we look young, beautiful, satisfied.

After all this, I pushed him away. Why? Because it was easy, and obvious, and there the story would end. No trauma. No chosenness. No selection. My tale would pale next to that of my parents, who had looked into the heart of darkness and lived, my mother banging pots and eating apples, my father fixing timepieces and chanting at the altar. My mother, it is true, was thrilled with Jacob—but the one I was trying to impress, all my life, was my father. He was my own private Selection Committee. Marriage at twenty-one, to a guy from a big house in the boroughs (with a country house in Connecticut)?

This, I think, was my mental reckoning:

Should I stay with, and soon marry, this wonderful guy, who wants to go to law school (that, or medicine, being the only choices then for a smart Jewish boy), comes from a nice Jewish family, understands me and my world, went to a yeshiva like mine, and will almost certainly be good to me for the rest of my life?

Nah.

Of course, I had loved being with Jacob and his parents, who instead of serving exhausted pasta with ketchup at dinner took me out to "fish restaurants" where you could get a "nice piece of sole" and a baked potato in foil, followed by a rich hunk of cheesecake. Other than the delis for hot dogs and a *greps* after our Doris Day ritual, my family had never "gone out" to restaurants, and on the very rare occasion that we went to a coffee shop, my mother would invariably help the busboy wipe the table. Jacob's mother, hair frosted in three shades of metallic blonde, would light up a post-fish Newport, exhaling like a movie star. His silver-haired, silver-moustachioed father (who actually looked like Mr. Lodge, Veronica's father) would unwrap a cigar with a great sense of quiet entitlement. And then we'd all get into the "champagne" colored Cadillac Eldorado and drive, soundlessly ensconced, to their sprawling Tudor-style "private house" in Forest Hills, Queens.

Jacob had a large backyard, with flagstone paving and a basketball hoop. He had a basement "rec room" with cork on the walls, lavender carpeting in the powder rooms (with matching monogrammed guest towels and mini soaps), a dining room as well as a citrus-colored "kitchenette," and a wood-paneled trophy room for all the father's philanthropic contributions to the Jewish world.

Sometimes the contrast between Jacob's upbringing and mine pained me. I once overheard his parents refer to my own tiny apartment as a "shoebox." My parents had invited them over to Washington Heights. Jacob's parents walked through the apartment (that would take about thirty seconds) and clucked about the two bedrooms, the one tiny baby blue bathroom with a sink that stood on skinny metal sticks, and the small kitchen. We had no dining room; we ate in the kitchen, at a small round table covered with a flowery oilcloth, its centerpiece a vase of plastic flowers. If you listened carefully, as you sat there, you could hear loud salsa playing out of someone's car radio. Dominicans and Colombians were joining the Puerto Ricans in my neighborhood, and now there were serious drug sales, there was frequent shooting.

Perhaps worst of all, Jacob's parents had bluntly asked that horror question: "So where does your brother sleep?"

"It's sort of a slum," they informed me, as we drove away in the Caddy, as though I could do something about it. Oh, is it? I'll move away at once! Thanks for letting me know! I'll move into something larger and more luxurious, in an expensive stylish neighborhood now!

I was both mortified and angry at them for belittling my parents. After all, we lived in Manhattan, even if it was the tip of the island, above uptown, above Harlem, at the end of the end of Ellington's "A" train. At least we didn't live in Queens! Slum-dwellers or not, we lived in THE CITY. But I had always wanted a quiet, gracious life, a childhood like Jacob had had, a garage with bikes and wooden sleds inside it.

I could have married this boy and had my own gracious home with wall-to-wall carpeting, an ecstasy of toilets, diamonds in my ears and circling my neck, not to mention a rock to weigh down my small-boned hand. I could have gone all Riverdale, and had pool parties and bridge nights like my mother's old friends. I could have gone to Junior's and had the maitre d' know how I liked my fish and my cheesecake.

Is this in the great tradition of the operatic movie magazines, which my mother and I both adored? Is it to defy my mother—who warned, like Cassandra: "A goy will hurt you. Watch out!" Am I trying to be heroic, jump into the subway tracks, join the Lithuanian army, like my father? Or is it simply the case that troubled people who have had a taste of hell are most familiar to me? The ambivalent, the torn, the wounded—these are my true fellow travelers, even as I get my A's at school. I like the minor keys, the complex atonalities.

I eventually find it impossible to stay with Jacob, the good boy, the Likable Kid who is close to his parents. Who has a vintage collection of baseball cards, including Mickey Mantle, Roger Maris, and Whitey Ford. Who will end up as a leading litigator in a prominent Jewish law firm—which is to say, a top firm in New York. Who offers me an amazing Tiffany solitaire at the Rainbow Room. He is gorgeous in a tux, and I wear the diamond for a short while, pondering normalcy, safety. My mother draws the relieved conclusion from this that her willful daughter's life is settled; she is ecstatic and starts buying me pots and pans that I, too, can clatter in the morning.

There were, however, things on my mind beyond domestic closure. All these years, I had been frustrated not to be going to Yale University, where my high school had put me forward as the top candidate. My grade point average had been something like 99.9 (nines repeating into infinity). My SAT's were perfect (Soloveitchik had taught me nothing if not how to study). Yale, thrillingly, had just begun opening its doors to women. I would have been one of the first pioneers to break into that hallowed men's world.

My father, I thought, would be thrilled by this opportunity. Wasn't he his daughter's biggest booster? Surprisingly, he had begged me to stay in New York. This meant that I would go to Barnard College (its brother, Columbia, unlike Yale, did not yet accept women). I would not go away to New Haven and prove myself equal to its deliciously intimidating traditions and/or decadent, entitled poseurs. I would not be a Jew among Wasps, a woman among men. I would not even leave home.

My incredulous high school headmaster had called my father. No one had ever passed up an opportunity to study in Cambridge or New Haven before. And the school wanted to keep its "spot" at Yale—at least one student a year.

"Mr. Taitz. We are convinced that your daughter's talents and ambitions would be best served by Yale University. Please strongly consider sending her there. This opportunity will change the course of her life."

"Yes. I will think about it," my father said.

After a day or so, he called me into the kitchen to talk.

"This Yale they talk about is a wonderful school, I am sure," he said, over a glass of tea. "World-famous, they tell me."

"Yes—and they've just started letting girls in—"

"And you, my talented little girlie, would be very successful if you went there. There is nothing I want more for you than to succeed in the world. But the Barnard College is also very good."

"It's so much easier to get into!"

"Maybe so. But it has something Yale does not have."

"What?"

"It is close to home. I don't want you to go far from me."

That was the problem. I wanted to break free.

"I have never asked you anything like this before, and this might surprise you. I'm not a beggar, and I don't like to impose on you. But you are the light of my life, and I want to see you as much as I can before I die."

You're dying? I thought, alarmed. It was true that besides the terrifying acromegaly that had changed his body, he had also had bleeding ulcers throughout the past years. Ironically, the intense use of aspirin during his painful years, in which his head had ached and his joints had creaked and grown, had caused much of his stomach to be destroyed. A few years earlier, much of it had been removed—months, they said, before internal bleeding would have killed him. Now, touching his fragile stomach, eyes shining, he continued.

"You know I am not so healthy now, I feel weaker every year. I don't know how many more years God will be good enough to grant me. So it is my deepest wish that you stay longer in New York. You have time to go away later. Please, Sonia, will you do as I ask of you?"

Of course, I had to say "yes." How could I add to the pain of a man who had lost his father to the Cossacks, his watch stores and prize Harley to the Communists, his mother to the Nazis—a man who had suffered with his wife, his son, the English language, acromegaly, and bleeding ulcers?

By senior year, however, I was determined to get away,

and to Yale itself if at all possible. My college advisor told me that my academics would be perfect for law school there, or at Harvard. She'd gripped my arm with go-get-'em fervor. So I had places to go and things to do, the special things that lucky, smart people in America do. I pictured arrival at Yale Law as the opening of golden gates into a sanctum sanctorum.

Now, I preferred the uniqueness of "Sonia" to any Susie or Sherri or Sandy. I loved my black hair, and I wore as much black to match it as possible. I wanted to expand, to break out of normal categories. I wanted to know the secrets of those who were extraordinary. I was in love with the ideas of existentialism, art, decadence, the French, Bertolucci, Rimsky-Korsakov. I loved the Russian nonhero Oblomov, who never got out of bed, the tortured Raskolnikov, and the simple, almost sardonic Candide, whom nothing on this earth really pleases.

I am sorry to say that my breakup with Jacob crushed him for a time. This once-happy person had truly loved me. He had never caused me a moment's pain, and I repaid him with rejection and wanderlust. I saw people like him, and marriages to people like him, as unworthy of my true intricacy. What a snob I was, always wanting to go to a place beyond mere contentment, to be "special." It seems so silly now, so very Third Reich of me, to divide the world into what was extraordinary (and to be breathlessly chased) and what was ordinary (and to be discarded).

Jacob called me, begging me to explain why it was over.

I told him that I loved him, but wanted something more out of life. I was, after all, still only twenty years old.

"What more do you want, Sonia? What?"

I didn't have the words then, but now I think I was looking for a long, played-out opera in an exotic setting with strict (maybe impossible) academic and social challenges. There, and there alone, my pain would evolve into a transcendent aria in the last act. It would be followed by applause (which I could feel, like Helen Keller, with my whole body), the love of multitudes, the wash of cleansing tears. Not to mention the healing sex that would follow a moment like that, on a ripped-down velvet curtain. And the illustrious career that would perpetuate my blissful immunity from the thorns of life.

Yes, Jacob was better off without a nut like me, but he didn't know that yet.

He was crying, and I was listening on the other end of the line. Suddenly, his mother grabbed and held the phone. They seemed to be wrestling, her fist on the mouthpiece, and I could hear muffled screams:

"ARE YOU STILL TALKING TO THAT BITCH? HANG UP!!"

Jacob was, of course, stronger than his mother. He grabbed the phone back from her and told me one last thing.

"I could have made you happy," he said, his voice low and threatening. "But now, now you'll never know."

Miles to Go

JACOB DID MAKE ME HAPPY, and much after him has been unhappy, but happiness was not what I was looking for. Happiness, I thought, was for losers and Lincoln Continental owners. My recess friend of long ago, Bunny Milcher, whose parents' greatest dream was to winter in Miami, had wanted to be "average and happy." Not me.

In my high school yearbook, we had all been asked to offer a quote, or a fragment of poetry, to go with our photograph. I had chosen a passage from Frost's "Stopping by Woods on a Snowy Evening." The lines, which mesmerized me, were:

The woods are lovely, dark and deep.
But I have promises to keep,
And miles to go before I sleep . . .

What miles? What promises? As my mother said about the runners up the hill—why do they run? What do they want? Had we been able to discuss it, she would have wondered: *Why* does Helen Keller have to go to Radcliffe? Why does she get onstage and talk like a deaf person, tapping her feet like a horse that knows the numbers? Why can't she just stay put and stop doing *meshugeneh kuntzen* (crazy tricks)?

She wondered the same about me. Why did I run? What did I want? I was her only daughter, meant to be her best friend. Why was I so strange? Whenever I did something that was not to her liking—and breaking it off with Jake was not to her liking—she would say, "You didn't get that from *me*." Meaning: your crazy, insatiable, promises-to-keep-and-miles-to-go personality—I don't like it.

Finding myself a Catholic boyfriend after the perfect Jacob was undoubtedly something Gita would have not have liked, had I ever told her. But it seemed a natural and necessary step in my road away from ease and familiarity. It seemed a direct consequence of my father's bravado and success with the threatening, larger world. I found my first real challenge right next door to me in our senior dorm at Columbia University.

Brendan Boyle O'Neill is my first romantic Radcliffe. He is often drunk, the worst thing that my mother had ever warned me about. ("Jews are not *shickers*.") When drunk, he calls me his "impossible Hebraic bitch"—"Watch, they'll call you a dirty Jew!" she had also cautioned—which only makes me laugh. What a nice adventure to see that some "goyim" really *do* drink a lot, and that when they do, they *do* talk, almost licentiously, about your Jewishness! What a relief, to cross these boundaries, to break these taboos and confront these fears!

And this Irish boy is somehow familiar and familial to me. Brendan's hair is black, like mine, his face pale like mine, and his cheeks and lips are flushed with blood. His dorm room is black and red, and he is passion and precision, Jesuitical exactitude and keening violins. Brendan has eyebrows like Jack Nicholson's and a mouth like a wicked Cupid. He is hot and hostile, languid and passionate. There is no understanding him; he is an almost untamable creature. He is a grown-up Billy, my playground tormentor, the one who shoved dirt into my impossible Hebraic mouth.

Brendan's desire for me temporarily, fleetingly, alters him, and the game changes me, too. I develop—and have never lost—a love of the lovely failure, a nostalgie de la boue. I think of dying for him, dropping off my Jewish perfection pedestal and into a state of luscious entropy.

He is a classics scholar, a boy from an elite Catholic prep school right across the street from my own East Side Jewish one. At Columbia he reads Greek and Roman, he quotes Ovid and Sophocles. I appreciate his learnedness; yeshiva made me a linguist and a textual analyst, too. He is intricate, a Dionysian Talmudist. We meet at the Metropolitan Museum, among the orange and black urns commemorating eternal strength and beauty. He is a black and orange urn to me, emblem of a timeless passion.

Brendan tells me that he knows he will die young, strong, and beautiful. I am mesmerized. He kisses me after he says this, and I don't want the kiss to end. I want to keep it alive, I want to keep him alive. The fact that our breaths must part inflames me. Despite my courtesanal façade, he is the first man I actually desire. Now I understand the dark, lustful feelings I have long (and calculatedly) inspired in others. Now there is no calculation; now there is instinct and wildness—all new to me, and soon as necessary as air. Also new to me is the pain that such feelings can cause, a new pain that makes the divide between the sexes seem as unbridgeable (and as necessary for me to bridge) as that between one people and another.

When Brendan is drunk, he talks like a genius, slowly, with slurred but at the same time carefully pronounced words that thrill me (my father has never been drunk, nor has Jacob). His mother punished him harshly throughout his childhood—he is often in a deep, untouchable state of apartness. She often put him in the closet where he sobbed and then was still.

So bring him to me, the big healer.

That is my motto. My heart is a tuning fork to those who have been hurt. The tired, the lonely, the hungry, the poor. Bring them to me, and I will tame these wounded creatures. Journey to my shores, welcome to my tent of love and surrender. Look how they rest their lunatic-lover-poet heads on my breasts. Look how they don't want to roam anymore, or bite anyone. I am a danger-tamer.

Frighteningly, Brendan wants to see my apartment up in Washington Heights. I suppose in some ways I am as exotic to him as he is to me. I try to talk him out of it, sure that a view of our humble abode of chicken fat and *Fiddler* albums will not add to the turn-on package I have so carefully created. But no.

The deep, sonorous tones of the Westminster chimes within my parents' apartment, which sound every fifteen minutes, have made a lasting impression on him. Whenever I have gone home for holidays and the occasional Sabbath dinner, I've called Brendan, and although I can no longer really hear this deep-voiced clock, although I am inured to its ceaseless accounting of the hours, Brendan has become enchanted by the sounds, particularly when we talk at midnight, which is often when we talk. After the usual, long introduction to the full hour, the Westminster chimes toll heavily, twelve times. Each tone reverberates over and over, overlapping the previous one, lingering to the next. It is a languid, continuous river of time:

Bong . . .

Bong . . .

Bong . . .

Bong . . .

Bong . . .

Bong . . .

Bong . . .

God, it does take forever when you notice it.

"Brendan?" I say, in the night.

"Shhh . . ."

Bong . . .

Bong . . .

Bong . . .

Bong . . .

"Brendan?"

Bong . . . .

"What?"

"I don't think you should come over here."

"Why? Are your parents that old-fashioned?"

"Yes."

"Do they hate me because I am a *goy*?" he says, and I can hear him smile, enjoying the full flavor of this Jewish word, so absurd and "ethnic" to him.

"No, but they would mind if they knew we were together."

Both my parents have lectured me since childhood about how much I need to restore and perpetuate our ravaged people. They want me to marry a Jewish man and have lots of Jewish children to restore the lost six million. They have told me stories about parents who have refused to attend their children's weddings to non-Jews. The scene in *Fiddler* in which one daughter marries a non-Jew and is banished is not entirely dated. To traditional, war-torn parents, these renegade children are almost as bad as the pogroms or Hitler. The choices they make reduce and destroy the Jewish people. They are, in short, traitors deserving excommunication.

Every time I have heard these moral tales, a part of me has discounted them. I know that with the Orthodox, the mother's religion determines that of the child. Any child of mine would thus be Jewish, no matter whom I married. By marrying "out," I could even add an ally to the poor, beleaguered tribe, drawing into its circle an invulnerable man who would be my husband and my children's father. This is my private survival algorithm: Jew plus non-Jew equals safety. And not just safety in numbers. Real safety. I always imagine a blue-eyed hero, rushing in to turn back the clock and save the lost.

Not that Brendan personifies any kind of practical plan. I'm dipping my toe into the waters of the exogamous, and the waters happen, in this case, to be part of a maelstrom. Now he wants to charge into my world before I'm ready.

"Could I come over when they're not there?"

"I guess," I hesitate, thinking of the tiny two-bedroom with the plastic on the couch, and the sofa bed that was my brother's small domain. Manny is now independent; he is in law school and has his own place, but Brendan knows he exists and will ask, like everyone else, where his room is.

"What is it? You sound sad."

"Me? No, it's fine." I'm also thinking about the knick-knacks and doodads from our first trip to Israel and my parents' subsequent trips there. There are big wooden plaques on the wall, three-dimensional folk carvings of people carrying grape-bunches on their shoulders. There are circular metallic plates, which contain, within them, the Hebrew words: *Chai* (life) and *Bracha* (blessing). There are olivewood coasters and knife sets, prominently displayed in the living room, as though they were treasures instead of ubiquitous tourist kitsch. To my parents, these mementos are priceless; they speak of life and art and industry in the Holy Land. But what will they look like to a classics scholar who frequents not only the Metropolitan Museum but also the Frick?

"No, no, it's fine," I say; I never let anyone know how sad or difficult anything is, or how freakish my lot. It's fine, come right in, I'm perfectly happy taking on the weight of the world as well as normal people's opinions on that weight and how I take it on.

Will Brendan meet my now totally bald father, with the weird, large-featured face and deep voice, wearing a sleeve-less undershirt (the better to reveal his frightening arms and shoulders) and a belted pair of trousers? Will he greet my damp-faced, round-cheeked mother in her housedress, wearing pink kid *shlurkes* on her feet as she spreads the dust around with a lint cloth or boils up some exhausted white chicken?

Despite my misgivings, which of course I can't express, we agree to come over after classes on a weekday.

So in we walk, just as the clock tolls five. Brendan, slim-hipped and cool in jeans and a black T-shirt, heads straight over to the breakfront, which covers most of one wall in the living room. How could he not? When you enter the apartment, it's half of what you see. The other half, on the opposite wall, is that plastic-smothered sofa. This day I notice that even the plastic is, if this is possible, worse-looking than ever—it is yellowed and cracking.

Brendan looks surprised by what he sees. He must realize that the stately sounds he has heard for months never emerged from a huge, strong grandfather clock, but from a mantel clock atop a walnut wall unit. It's something like hearing deafening croaks from the side of a body of water. Sure that you've found a proud, frightening, and perhaps primeval life-form, you search for the source of the sound— and it's only a wee bullfrog, lonely, calling for a mate.

"*This* is the clock that makes all the chimes?"

"Yep."

"You know, the deep tolling sounds—"

"Yep. I know the sounds. This is it."

This is it. This is me; this is the shit-hole ghetto I temporarily crawled out of. I am the lonely wee bullfrog. Brendan lets his dark blue eyes travel around, surveying my poverty. Standing in that room, he has already taken in a large share of the apartment. There is only a kitchen, a master bedroom, my sliver of a room, and a tiny bathroom with light blue tiles of which I used to be proud.

"Wow. Everything's so small here."

"Yep."

Amid my shame, I feel bad for my mother. She thought our living room was elegant and sophisticated. Look at the bronze-colored, thick, wall-to-wall carpet. Look at the coffee table, shaped like an oval, beveled glass on top of walnut (to match the breakfront). Appreciate the matching lamps, with their frosted globes of deep yellow glass. Each one twists on its own stalk in a very modern way. Look at the drapes, ivory, with green patterns like Greek keys. Like Greek keys,

Brendan, you classics major! And even though the sofa is covered with plastic, look at its elegant bone-whiteness, its precious threads of gold. It is only in plastic to protect its fragile beauty. Look at the square pillows, with buttons in their center, like accepting friends. The pillows are gold, too; can't you see they match everything?

But Brendan's eyes are fixed on this breakfront. Now I see what he sees. In the very center of the massive wall unit, in the place to which we never really pay attention, there is a "slide-out bar." When you pull open the glass doors, a light goes on, like magic. Then you can see a cunning array of little stemmed glasses, party-pretty and delicate, a few short glasses, and two snifters. You can slide these glasses out, lift them out of the shallow, green velvet circles in which they stand. The whole display reminds me of the showcases at my parents' store, rarely opened, the contents rarely dislodged, and then only for a buying customer.

"What kind of booze do you have?" Brendan's eyes brighten with pleasure.

"What kind of—"

"Do you have any gin?"

"What kind?" I'm stalling. Of course we don't have any gin! We're Jews!

"Gilbey's? Bombay? Tanqueray?"

Brendan is really fluent in a language I don't speak.

"Uh, no, I don't think we have . . . um . . ."

I slide open one of the large rectangular drawers on each side of the breakfront. Here, packed in next to my parents few records and my brother's many rock albums, is where I know they keep the liqueurs and the schnapps for special occasions. The only time I've seen my father drink is the obligatory four cups at a seder (and he prefers grape juice to wine), or at the synagogue, toasting the Sabbath with a tiny plastic cup of Manischewitz and a square of sponge cake, or, very occasionally, having a glass of good brandy.

"Hey, look!" I say, affecting cheer. "Would you like some slivovitz? And—what's this—oh, this is good—Cherry Heering? It tastes like cherries, but it's—it's got quite a little kick—"

My mother offers this to her fanciest guests, say if the ones from Riverdale were to visit for some reason. Out would come the Cherry Heering, imported from Denmark. The men would have slivovitz, an old-world shot of pure alcohol, flavored with plum.

"You must be kidding."

"No, uh uh, I'm serious."

"No scotch? No gin? No tonic?"

I'm not sure what tonic is, exactly, but remind him that he can always have some seltzer water. We always have that.

"And here's something I bet you never had," I add, still trying to act excited about ravaging my parents' things.

I pick up a liqueur that is housed in something shaped like a genie's bottle. The label is a beautiful, Eilat-stone turquoise, mixed with gold.

"What on earth is that?" Brendan smiles, laughs a little. "It really looks tacky. And you know I hate sweet drinks."

"It's Sabra, the liqueur of Israel." The bottle is at least a decade old; a little primordial stickiness from the last use keeps me from easily opening it.

"Would you help me twist this off?"

I hand the bottle to Brendan, who takes it up with a trace of his smirk, and tries to pry open the glucose-glued top.

This is what my mother sees when she enters the house:

Me and a boy, a boy with hair as black as mine, about to

share a nip of Sabra, Israel's contribution to the world of liqueur.

To my great relief, she smiles encouragingly at me, as though to say:

Nice setup. Another guy came running up the hill. And this one is handsomer than the last one. And what's wrong with a little drink from Israel at the end of the day. It could be very pleasant.

Meanwhile, I'm thinking: Brendan-the-goy can pass!

"You're home early," I say, casually. Brendan is still working with the cap. With one final twist, he sets the genie bottle free.

"Mazel tov!" says my mother.

"L'chaim!" says Brendan, merrily, again with that little laugh.

"So give me just a little, and what is your name?"

Taking a crystal stemmed glass out, Brendan pours my mother a drop of the elixir of Israel. He is smart enough to hesitate about his name, because Brendan is not the most Semitic name anyone can ever think of.

I help out: "His name? *Bernard* is his name."

Brendan laughs again. It's such a bad name for him. Bernard. Bernie. But my mother smiles her approval. She can see me married to a Bernard, maybe even this Bernard, this happy laugher.

"So, Bernard," she confides to him, "the butcher had a problem today, he can only deliver before six o'clock, so I ran early out of the store, and—"

Brendan hands her a delicate stemmed glass full of Sabra.

"Bernard, you should have some, too," I point out.

"Well, I hate to drink too much—I just thought *you* wanted some."

"No—*you* did!" I pour him a glassful, full to the rim to punish him for those laughs.

"So now, again, a real L'chaim," my mother says, taking a small bird sip and waiting until Brendan does the same.

"It's good, no?"

"Uh, oh, yes," says Brendan.

My mother gives me her glass. "Here, Sonialeh, finish, for me it's too much. And your last name?" she continues, now to Brendan, as she bustles away into her bedroom to change out of her work clothes.

"My—my last name?" he repeats.

The house is so small she could probably hear us if we whispered, so I mime "Don't say anything!" to Brendan. I can Judaize his name. I will *kasher* him like meat is made kosher, by putting sea salt into it so all the blood and wildness runs out. Just give me a minute. O'Neill. O'Neill. No, I can't. Most names, you could add "witz" or "berg," or even "insky" or "itsky"—but O'Neill is an insurmountable challenge.

"It's actually O'Neill." I call out boldly. "Like the Irish name."

"Oh," she says, returning, popping shut the last snap of her daisy-patterned housedress. "A lot of people say I look Irish."

That's true. With her green eyes, cherry cheeks and auburn hair, Gita could pass for a colleen, and it flatters her (in the way that my own Jewish looks do not). The Irish, in fact, are among the non-Jews she least fears. They are a people who have struggled, like the Jews; like the Jews, they have made an art form of their suffering. And she thinks they are good-looking, which they are.

"Yes, well, Brend—*Bernard's* father is from Ireland. But

he met a nice Jewish girl here in New York, and guess what, he converted."

"And they raised you Jewish, Bernie?"

"I'm as kosher as a Hebrew National hot dog," says Brendan, whom I could have kicked.

"Not to mention the knish," he adds, piling it on. "Which I like with mustard."

My mother is more warmed up by the minute.

"And do you like the Sabra?" she says,

"The wh—"

"Look, you didn't drink anything. I guess you have your mother's genes. We Jews, we're really not drinkers."

My mother truly liked Brendan and was actually a bit forlorn when we parted ways. I was headed, after all, to law school after college. I had places to go, things to do, and miles to go before I slept. And Brendan's constant state of arch drunkenness really began to annoy me.

Omega and Alpha

A s THE SONG at the '64 World's Fair had declared:
"There's a Great! Big! Beautiful! Tomorrow!"

I had long seen that Great Big Beautiful Tomorrow on the horizon. It now involved my becoming a powerful being of irrelevant gender. ATTORNEY AT LAW, the sign would now say, gold-shaded black letters on a wooden square, like my father's OMEGA sign.

My father had always wanted me to be successful, and to him (as to my college advisor), the Juris Doctor degree represented the apex of American vision. How many presidents and heads of industry had been lawyers? How many senators and CEOs and "partners"? What immigrant's child would say no to a salary of $100,000, rising to a possible million or more at the end of seven years? And how much power did those numbers imply? As long as I succeeded, my parents' life-long struggles would have been meaningful. They had been kicked around their whole lives, but now their child would wear the "brass buttons"—my father's phrase for those in power. I could go up to all oppressors, shove my nose in their faces, and say, with authority:

"Hey buddy, now stop picking on my folks, it's enough already. Check out Rule #5485, subsection 719. It's about time to stop being mean. Or do you want me to sue you? Because I could. I am, after all, an attorney at law."

That I was a woman about to say "Hey, buddy," etc. did not matter in the least—my father was feminist when it came to me, to a fault. "Any cow can have a baby," he had once said. Now feminism seemed to be agreeing. Merely to procreate, to sit home and lactate? We can do more than that. We can accomplish things, both at home (boy-girl twins, delivered vaginally and sans drugs) and in the "real" world (corner office would be good). We can have it all! Better to go to law school, then, and tough it out like a real man. Or tougher, like an alpha woman in a man's world.

With my transcript, as my advisor had said, I could anticipate being admitted to Harvard or Yale. Yale, to which I had longed to go before, and now to enter its most competitive bastion . . . irresistible. And Harvard Law, the stuff of legend (mostly unpleasant, but of course that only attracted me): the place in which, in one famous film, a dour professor asks his poor students to look left and right—only one will survive. How concentration-campish! I apply to both and am accepted to both. A primal moment of "*Yes.*" I've won the American lottery. In my first real "selection," I have made the fateful cut.

I remember doing an ecstatic victory dance in my room. I jump up and down like a winner on a game show; I do the twist, the pony, and the swim. I guess a part of me had always wanted those "brass buttons." Now I would be among the rule-makers (not just the rule-maker's favorite). I would be safe, and I would make others safe, leading them out of Egypt, Babylon, Persia, and Poland.

But why is it that, when I visit the Harvard Law campus, all my fellow overachievers seem on the verge of a break-down? There is talk of first-years attempting suicide, of students tearing pages out of library books so that others can't study from them and "ruin the curve." One student, a tall, storky girl, whispers fiercely to me as I pass, "Save yourself! Don't come here!"

Yale Law seems mellower, and it is smaller—only 150 people in my year, half of them women. "Seventy-five women from all of America," I think, as if all of America is applying, en masse, to beef up its credentials. The few students I talk to seem breezy—off to play tennis doubles, or to attend some graduate lecture on Kant and the categorical imperative. At least, that is how it appears to me on my first visit to the legendary, longed-for New Haven, Connecticut.

"It's the school of Athens," I reassure myself, alluding to the vanished world in which scholars promenaded and thought deep thoughts, philosopher-kings all. Leaping forward a few centuries, I continue to fantasize: "It's the Renaissance in Florence. I could go there and write, read French romantic poetry and Russian novels. I'm sure that's what everyone does at a place like this." I look forward to evenings discussing decadence or existentialism with my ultra-clever new law buddies, followed by an evening with a Kama Sutra expert with a brain.

"It's probably the best school in the United States of America," I tell my father upon acceptance. He cannot be more proud, and makes the following speech: "I kept you back in New York City for your college, but now you must go forward towards your future."

OK, I nod, thinking that it's about time. And Yale isn't that far away.

He isn't finished.

"I have always worked hard, like a dog. Day and night, I drove myself, and I got sick, and sometimes the sweat would pour from me, and still I kept going. Do you know why? Of course you know, I have always told you. So that you could accomplish anything you wanted. What you learn in your head, no one can ever take from you. No one could pay for me to go to school, but I will always support your goals, even if I have to keep on working forever so you could reach your potential and become a real somebody. This is my privilege and my joy.

"So go now, my Karaputzi," he says, ruffling my hair. "Go to your success."

"Thanks, Daddy."

We were often, apparently, on the same page in the manual for upwardly striving, dream-seeking immigrants. I had my hubris, and he his innocent belief that there was a life-long prize at the end of the finish line. All I had to do was get there and collect my reward. A modern story of redemption.

The problem was, I soon came to realize, what did American "redemption" mean? The alien new language I heard when I enrolled on campus immediately disturbed me: Big bucks. Arugula. Humidors. Souffle. Brooks Brothers. Shrimp cocktail. Chablis. Clerkships. Six figures. High-powered. Antitrust. No trust. Get it in writing, in triplicate form.

And the courses: Contracts, Torts, Evidence. "Business Units."

With a flip of my stomach, I quickly realized that I did not want any of this business. I hated what it stood for. The law itself, and its rigidities, were foreign to me. I had had my taste of culture, art for art's sake, passion and intellectual searching. Was this to be the end of my brief expansion from the veal box? Was it all now to be bills of lading and temporary injunctions? Was this my reward for studying like a lunatic for the last fifteen years? Membership in some corny golf club where the men wore bright green pants and discussed train accidents and "preferred" shares?

In class, I entertained myself by daydreaming about the personal, supposedly irrelevant, part of each law case. If the "fact pattern" was about the apples that fell into Mr. Jones's yard from Mrs. Smith's tree, I wanted to know what kind of apples. Tasty or rotten? Mealy or crisp? McIntosh (my mother's favorite)? Were Mr. Jones and Mrs. Smith young and virile? Having an affair, I suppose? And why not? Life was short and boring. I felt a kind of perverse pride when my first-year contracts professor, the redoubtable Grant Gilmore, wrote on my paper: "Full of brilliance, nonsense, and mistake." I loved the distinction between mere mistake and total nonsense. He understood my mind as well as anyone. I was once thought to be brilliant, the law was nonsense, and my coming here, of all places, had been a big mistake.

Here we were, stuck in torts when it was autumn outside and real apples were ripening, heavy-falling; you could fill a basket with them. Latin phrases, pouring into our heads like wet cement into molds, also intrigued me, if only in their creative misuse. *Res ipsa loquitur* (the thing speaks for itself). What thing? The thing that rises when a pretty girl goes by? The heart that beats faster? These things speak for themselves, but who among these scribbling note-takers and nitpickers is listening? *Habeas corpus* (you have the body). Yes, I *did* have the body, and it was young and passionate, so what was it doing in this dusty Gothic classroom?

What were these cases, this Latin, this game? How did law manage to ruin the world, replacing truth and beauty with a poorly fitting grid? How did language itself suddenly become so limited, cold, and formal? Was all that preceded this profession merely a juvenile stage, a suggestively inspiring course in college, a romantic folly, to be discarded for less childish things at the appropriate age? I did not want to be left behind on the failure train. When college ended, I had fears of going back to Washington Heights, my mother's onion-potato kitchen and my own set of pans. I didn't want to be sent to the wrong line—the death line, then heaped in a pile. I wanted to strive, to win. But what was this prize, and why was it so horribly wrong for me?

I had never fallen down before. I had fought the acknowledgment of sadness all my life, and here it was, an enveloping shroud. My familiar, the savage god who cornered me. Now, unable to enjoy my torts or my tarts, I tumble down a well. It is almost luxurious, an Alice-fall where everything becomes possible after you topple in. I let go of my end of the bargain of survival.

A covenant, I thought, had been made with me, as it had been with Israel. Be good, be true, be special—and you will get to the Promised Land.

But that was not going to be possible, not here.

This was where my own journey began. My father, like my mother, knew little about me and what I needed. Immigrants' children did not usually become writers, thinkers, and artists; that life was unpredictable. Success could never be guaranteed. So they went to law school/med school/business school and made their parents proud. Now that I was at the top and had looked at the view, I saw the wrong land. My parents, who had never surrendered to despair, would have been ashamed of me—if they had sensed anything about my feelings.

Couldn't I go back down the mountain and start again, start at the place where I was a free child, not tied to a Bubbe, not darkened by six million murders? I wanted paintings, sixty-four colors, avant-garde theater, English literature. I wanted orchestras and arias; I wanted to read rapaciously and write my own bold words. I wanted truth and beauty; I wanted textured Old Europe and its ivory keys and golden mantle of culture. More than anything, I wanted to participate, and be loved, in my own true identity.

I should have listened to my mother, who loved flowers and fresh, ripe tomatoes and her little apartment that gave her joy. She is the one who, whenever I told her how tough the professors were, how pressured the world I had entered, would answer, simply:

"Let them *plotz*." (Explode.) How wise she was.

She would have been happy if I had simply wanted to stay with her a few hours every day, and make some wonderful soup, redolent with dill and bay leaves. Or eat a *shtickl* pound cake, drink a glass of tea with honey. We could have enjoyed the little things together, flowers (plastic maybe, silk if we were lucky, but *flowers*), pushed and pulled our wagons up and down the avenues hunting for the best and cheapest apples and tomatoes and cantaloupe. But at that that point, chicken soup, honeyed tea, and apples were the last things on my hubris-warped mind. I didn't like law, but I would not come home.

MY BROTHER, meanwhile, has started a new, exciting life as a lawyer in California. On a trip out west to check out summer internships, I visit with Manny. His light and airy "garden apartment," with its patch of grass and a lemon tree, is as antithetical to my parents' old-world ambience as Westwood is to Washington Heights.

He drives me around in a rented blue convertible. We drive up hills and down thrilling canyons. Manny is tan and muscular, more handsome and long-haired than ever. His bell-bottoms are cleverly worn out, and he wears them low on his hips. As our car circles up toward the glass aeries of millionaires and movie stars, my brother asks if I would like to see anyone's home.

"You—you know these people?"

"Well, no, but you don't have to know them to—"

"Do you know where Elizabeth Taylor lives?"

"Eliz—nah! It's not like that. Who cares about the stars? You don't have to be such a tourist! It's like heaven here. Everyone's so open and friendly. You just ring the doorbell and they let you in."

"Really?" Back in Washington Heights, our door had three Medeco locks and a chain. Before letting anyone in, my mother would ask, with a put-upon, almost terrified timbre: "Who *is* it??" And even when she got her answer the chain would stay on until she had peered for a good minute through the little peephole.

"Los Angeles isn't full of worries and hang-ups like New York," my big brother is explaining. "Where we come from, yeah, everyone is uptight and farkrimt," he says, meaning that their faces are pursed and pruned as though they'd tasted too much bitterness to loosen up.

"Oh, I know. You don't have to tell me how farkrimt they are."

"Well, little sister. It's just a different world here."

Manny pulls up to a mansion that seems to teeter on the edge of a cliff. He opens his car door and gets out, and I follow him to the huge wooden front doors of this palace.

He must have rung a silent bell that I didn't even notice, because after a minute or so the doors swing open to reveal acres of white marble on the floor, polished smooth as a skating rink. I peer in—just beyond, past another pair of impressive doors (glass, French), lies a pale blue pool that stretches into the pale blue horizon, cool as nothingness.

The woman who has opened the door has long, brown hair. She is barefoot, and on her big toe is a shining diamond. Tanned and slightly worn, she is dressed in a sheer Grecian gown, under which we can see a black bikini with gold straps. From the way she looks at my brother, you would think she knew him for a long time.

"Hey," she says, with an unnatural (to me) happiness.

Yes, I said it. Happiness is kind of unnatural to me, and not only in Los Angeles. But I could get used to it. I am having fun. I want to go into her kitchen—it's probably vast—and ask for a dish of strawberry ice cream. With a maraschino cherry, my mother's touch of luxury.

"Hi," my brother is saying. "Wow. My little sister here and I—well, we were driving around your neighborhood, and we noticed your lovely home."

"Oh, thanks, uh huh?"

"Yes, well, my sister, she's from New York."

Manny and the barefoot Grecian lady exchange sympathetic glances.

"Oh . . ."

"Yeah, I know," he says. "Can I show her how people live out here?"

As though everyone in Los Angeles lived on cloud nine.

She did. Her furniture is all soft and white (without plastic). A large wolfhound pads about lazily. The lady's feet, though shoeless, seem small and soft. Past the white marble, there is thick white carpeting, and past that, around the pale blue pool, an exquisite orangy tile that rhymes with the sunlight.

"Thanks for your hospitality!" my brother says, as he slams the car door. I look behind me as we whirl down the hills, but the house vanishes into a swirl of yellow dust and tenacious cactuses.

Even my law firm interviews in Los Angeles had an unsprung feeling to them. One of them, conducted toward the end of the day, ended with me and several other candidates for a summer associateship herded into a hot tub, bobbing like dumplings under the stars. A partner passed us flutes of champagne whose bubbles mingled with Jacuzzi foam.

If that didn't want to make you leave your worries behind and start fresh, what could?

But I still had this sense of "promises to keep." What did that mean? I didn't know. But I didn't think it meant sipping Premier Cru or cooking like a matzoh ball in a vat of boiling water. Even the lure of entertainment law (where I could meet someone like Liz) was not enough. My brother had traveled west and found freedom in its lack of history, its open, sunny acceptance. I, unable to settle, unable to rest, chose escape in another way—equidistant, and in the opposite direction.

Europe was full of history, turf wars, grudges, vendettas, pogroms. And if California was always sunny, England—I was soon to discover—offered a moody gray rain that never seemed to stop.

From the time of my early disaffection with law, I had toyed with the idea of transferring to Oxford or Cambridge to study literature. Many of my law colleagues had gone there for extra degrees before stepping up to the practical rigors of American jurisprudence.

"Eeew! Why would you go there?" said a dissenting law school friend, who had actually turned down a Rhodes scholarship after visiting the boggy campuses of Oxford and Cambridge.

"It smells like rotten milk and Lysol," another, who had been there, insisted. "No one has a chin, the food reeks of boiled cabbage and rotting pig, and the men are all gay. You can't be serious."

Oh, I am serious; I have made a radical decision. I have applied and been accepted to Oxford to study nineteenth-century English literature. To my parents' consternation, I plan to become my true self there, and even to write. After only one year of law school, I have decided to cross the ocean, eastward. Now, I have secured a berth, student passage, on the regal vessel *QE II*, named after England's reigning monarch.

In this mid-Atlantic limbo, past and present seem to flip-flop. As though we already were in the nineteenth century, people voluntarily sit on the windy deck, wrapped in coarse blankets and drinking beef bouillon. Or endless milky cups of tea, in thin bone china. I read Dickens on deck. Time moves counterclockwise and I love it.

I am sailing away from everything I know. I am going to be alone and in a foreign land. I am not really reckless (though my mother doubts that). I am still a good and responsible girl. I have managed to fulfill all my first-year requirements. I have even obtained a bona fide leave of absence to go to Oxford from Yale's dean, a benevolent fellow with a broad mind.

According to my plan, I would enter Europe sitting proudly on my safe academic perch. These were the dangerous louts who had chased the Jews out, over and over, for centuries. Spain, home of the Inquisition. France, home of the Dreyfus trial and Vichy government. Germany, Poland, and Lithuania, my parents' country, all vying for the title of most bloodthirsty. England, which purged all its Jews in the twelfth century (with a spectacular rout at York), yet has nevertheless managed to produce literary grotesques like Shylock and Fagin out of a centuries-long, *Judenrein* vacuum. Who, as more recent fillip, patrolled Israel's harbor at a crucial time in the '40s, sending boatloads of Jews back to a sure death in the Old World.

So off I go, away from Big Dreams, Big Bucks, and Big Gulps, into an oddly provincial part of the bloody checkerboard. Perhaps God, as the psalm promised, *would* set a table for me in the presence of my enemies, the landed snobistocracy. I would graciously invite Europe to join me in eating—what would it be—chicken soup. And they would slurp it, love it, want more, and even ask me for the recipe. I would bring them vats of it, as my mother had done for Mrs. Shroodel on 172nd Street between Broadway and Fort Washington Avenue. And they would pat my head and give me hard candy with soft fillings. They would row my boat to safety, under the light of stars, and I would plant trees in their honor in the Avenue of the Righteous, in Jerusalem.

I do, of course, need my father's permission to leave law school and America. It is hard-earned.

This is how I explain it to the poor, long-suffering man:

"I want to learn more broadly. Law school is practical, but I have a deeper side to me."

It's an odd concept, but I know that my father has that deeper side within him, too. He nods thoughtfully.

"I don't want the dry Talmud and not the Torah, the polemics instead of the poetry. I want my knowledge pure and not relative to time and place and jurisdiction. I want to be a real scholar, not just a shallow businesswoman. Please give me one last chance to learn—really learn—at the oldest and most prestigious school in the world. Oxford University."

"Oxford? Yes, of course. I have heard of it," says my father.

"It is almost a thousand years old. Kings and—and *Sultans* have studied there." There's that Ahasuerus motif again, and I'm seeing myself in that paper crown and big plastic jewels that declare me a winner.

"It's the hardest school to get into, particularly for an American—and of all the schools in the world, it is the best."

I truly mean these simple, naive words. For me, Oxford would be the ultimate chosen place, the Promised Land of scholarship. This could be my true Radcliffe. Having majored in English literature at Barnard, I was dazzled by the idea of going to its source.

"I always worked hard for you," says my father, "and I always wanted you to have all your opportunities. I can see that you want this very much, my Karaputzi."

"It's the door I've been looking for. And after this, I'll go back to law school. I have an official leave. I can come back and finish"

"Yes, you must complete what you start. It is cowardly to quit."

I don't agree; sometimes quitting is heroic. I simply don't have the guts to let go of law school.

"I'll end up with two wonderful degrees, don't worry," is all I can say.

"Good. I think I will let you go to Oxford University."

But before I can relax, he adds:

"But first, I must ask you to make this vow to me."

The Vow

H ERE is my father's request:

"You must promise that no matter how far you go, what you experience and what you learn, you will remain faithful to your God and your people."

Long silence. I am thinking. He gives me time to consider my answer.

He is probably only talking about my inner identity. That is probably solid. I have been marked, by him and my mother, since birth. I know you cannot promise to keep believing something, but that is what we all do. We swear eternal love. We swear faith and allegiance to a country. We continue to pray when faith wavers. I believe in passionate avowals, but a part of me wants also to remain porous and open. I want to be touched by the new; otherwise, why travel at all? On the other hand, Jews have always traveled, yet managed to retain their identities. Somehow, no matter how long the axis, how far from the center it takes them, the center does hold true.

So although I find the question oppressive, and oppression antithetical to loyalty or love, I am able to be honest when I make the vow. I cannot fight the fact that I am Jewish. Indeed, I will fight the fight for the Jews. I will even look for the next fight so I can start fighting it. Let's face it: I went to Europe to open a dialogue. To resume the old fight that's never silent in my head. And in that sense, I am my father's most faithful daughter.

In the more conventional sense, however, I betray my father from the moment I enter the Sceptered Isle. I am finally, finally, outside their world. Intriguingly, I am also deep inside their past. Europe is the Old World, still holding to dark, creaky theories that cripple it. I can wrestle with, and perhaps subdue, my parents' and my people's atavistic nightmares of not belonging.

On top of which, the Old World, or what's left of it, is damnably beautiful. I can see the appeal of having your own country, which goes back for centuries, with history and banners and old mulled wine in stone pubs. I can see what joy there could be in being a native son. A horse, the saddle, the land, the trees . . .

So vow, shmow. It's not easy to stay sober in England, in any sense of the word. Despite its wetness—or perhaps because of the vagueness of water—the place is seductive. The Kingdom feels like this: haze of rain, smell of fireplaces, old rugs and sherry, leaded windows and cobblestone paths. Swans on the River Isis, flowing like white ribbons. Bicycles jingle, and punts sail slowly by, pushed by lanky, long-haired boys whose cheeks are flushed pink. Yes, it is all sensuous, and I start to loll immediately. The leather-bound books smell rich and savory, as do the pubs, with their loamy scent of spilled beer and cigarettes. Church bells toll in the misty air, lavender at dusk.

A few months after I arrive, I encounter an English actor on the Oxford stage. I am already well seduced by England's post-Raphaelite art, by dusty first editions, ancient carpets, and cool mini-flutes of sweet sherry. I have fallen deeply into

nineteenth-century English literature—Romantic poetry and
some of the world's greatest novels, turning page after magical page in a place where you could still smell the fireplaces
and climb the cold stone staircases, a past still gleaming
through the fog and mists. How hard did the wind have to
blow to tip me over? Not hard. And this man was a hurricane.

There he was, in flowing eighteenth-century wig and a
poet's shirt, playing the irresistible lover, Don Juan, in Moliere's
version of the legend. The play was performed when winter
thawed, when springtime brought intoxicating fragrances to
the countryside. There, at the Oxford Playhouse, professional
actors and equally brilliant students, members of the estimable
OUDS (Oxford University Dramatic Society), trod the boards
together, producing works of remarkable quality. I fell into a
deep obsession with this particular artist's long, strong frame,
sensuous mouth, satin shoes, and dandified wit. I loved the way
"Juan" tossed the women into his net, then discarded them. A
real courtesan like me would be more of a scene-partner for
him, I thought. So I had only one thought as I came back to
see this man onstage, over and over, like a stalker.

Bring him to me.

Here, my hormones averred, was my own alien king.
Here was my challenge. He was my prey, and I his. I determined to find my personal Don Juan.

I thought the man was a professional actor. He seemed
older than much of the cast—with his dark kohled, shadowy
eyes and decadent manner, he seemed to be at least thirty. I
asked student amateurs I knew if they had seen the play or
heard of its star performer. I searched all the directories to
find his address—Oxford, the nearby town of Reading, even
London and its suburbs. I could not find this name—an un-
usual name, though English.

And then, one day in college, I heard the porter at the lodge call out.

"Mr. Deards! Mr. Deards—if you please!"

When I turned, I saw a fleeting figure, flying by on his bicycle.

I asked the porter if the person he had called, the one who'd flown by, had indeed been the man I was looking for.

"Yes, Miss."

"Paul Deards, the—the actor?'

"Dunno about that, Miss. He lives here in St. Catherine's College, is all I know, and he's got a package from his mum."

A package from his mum? For Mr. Deards? Here?

"More often than not, it's biscuits. They'll keep, I expect."

Was I supposed to believe that the man of my dreams was a biscuit-eating student at my own college? The boys around here were thin and tiny, with amazingly spotty skin. Many actually had white-taped glasses and wore pen-holders, and they weren't in Halloween costume dressed as "nerds."

"Which staircase?" Each staircase led to a bunch of rooms.

"Staircase Seven."

That was *my* staircase!

"Which room?"

At this point, I really expected this Alice in Wonderland dream to continue with his saying, "*Your* room, Miss, check under the pillow!"

But, in fact, it was almost as good. Don Juan lived right below me.

I was already on top of him, I exulted internally!

Later that day, I knocked on his door.

A tall, gangly, and somewhat spotty blonde boy with lanky, flat hair stood there. He looked to be about eighteen or nineteen years old.

"Uh, I'm actually looking for Paul—Paul Deards?"

He stared at me somewhat coldly.

I repeated my sentence, and he said, "What about?"

Peering into the dorm room, I saw a variety of English types: the guy who sat in the corner, on the floor, intensely trying to play guitar chords, with a few straggly hairs growing out of his chin; the one with the really short bell-bottoms (they called them "flares") ending at his calf and revealing droopy gray socks; and the wizardy one with brown teeth and incredibly thin legs crossed at both knee and ankle. On one wall was a Snoopy poster; on the other, a tiny kitten swept up in a ladle over a bowl of chicken noodle soup, with the motto "Hang in There."

"I *could* be in the wrong place," I muttered, deflated by the creepy dreariness.

"Well, why are you looking for that bloke?" said Paul, finally.

"Because I think he is the best actor ever. Did you see him in—"

"Oh, yeh?" he interrupted, and yanked me into the room.

A few days later, he talked to me again. After supper, I saw him mount his bicycle, about to run off. He saw me and stopped.

"Hey! Care to come with me?"

"Where are you going?"

"Oh, I do this Suicide Center volunteering bit. Trying to keep the world going 'round, you know."

"I *do* know," I say, thrilled that he is open to the world of pain and sorrow.

"Would you like to have a look at the place? It's usually quite empty. Come along then, you can keep me company."

Not long after, at the Hotline, we are drinking hot cocoa and he is reciting poetry that he has written, odd William Blakean lines that mesmerize me. And I am telling him my stories, too.

I tell him about the Holocaust, which, strangely enough,

I have almost never talked about before. I tell him everything, because, after all, I am at the Suicide Hotline, the
very crossroads of the word *pain*. And the signs—including a big one on the entry door—say "We Can Carry Your
Load With You."

"That is so sad," Paul says, his eyes welling.

I stare into his wet blue eyes with my own wet browny-
green eyes.

"Would you like to sit on my lap?" he adds helpfully.

I am stunned; this seems unprofessional, but . . .

Oh, yes.

Then a kiss. I'm surprised at how shaky he is. After all,
he is an Englishman, and a Wasp. I really never understood
that Wasps could be so nervous, and I never knew they could
feel so . . .

More, please.

And that is how it begins.

When his next part is cast, I attend his performances not
as a guest but as an insider. It is *The Tempest*, and he is Caliban.

Paul chooses to play this role in green, even painting
his face and limbs the color of moss. The production takes
place at night. He appears with a swoosh—Caliban, the primal man, leaping from a tree and into the river, then onto
the stage. He shakes himself off like a dog and humps the
ground as he roars:

"I shall people all the world with Calibans!"

Can I come too?

After the play, we kiss and hug, and his green body paint
comes off on me. I think of Billy, the kid I loved at four, and
his primordial mud. I feel connected to Shakespeare, to art,
to passion, and to the pulse of the earth.

D URING THIS TIME, with me in England, and my brother
in Los Angeles, my father loses his store in what is now
Lincoln Center. "Taitz Jewelers" has been condemned by
the greed of a landlord, who raises the rent higher than my
parents—or any other small business—can ever afford.

My father has my mother write a special letter to me. He
is uncomfortable with writing in English.

> *Darling Sonia'le!*
> *Please do not worry. We are in big trouble, only you can help.*
> *Daddy wants you to write a letter to the important people, maybe*
> *newspapers, the Times, so everyone knows that we are being*
> *chased out of our store, no one does nothing we are worried.*
> *Please you are so smart help us find a way so we can earn our*
> *living we have worked so hard all our lives we don't deserve this.*
> *Your Loving Parents (Gita and Simon)*

I call them immediately, seeking more information. My father can only repeat an idée fixe: if they can save vanishing spe-

cies (his example is the crocodile), why not the old watchmakers, the skilled craftsmen and their handmade world? Inside his request is the familiar paradigm—I am about to be annihilated. I am not your father, but your child and your responsibility. It is your duty to save me. And only you, Sonia Judith Taitz (carrier of at least three dead people, and now two live ones) can do it.

So I use my words and write a letter about the Holocaust, about watchmakers and other dwindling craftsmen, and about vanishing species. I send it to various newspapers, but there is no response at all from anyone.

"They never stopped the trains to Dachau," my father tells me, over the phone lines from New York to Europe. "They never came. The world never cared. The British turned even Jews back to Poland," he reminds me, as I stand in Britain and talk to him. "You have to keep going. You have to care. Write something more."

I do care, but it is hard to have my words used, over and over, for someone else's purpose, and not my own. (This was also a problem at law school.) I want, for example, to write a letter to someone, anyone, seeking peace from the chore of being my parents' alarm system and conduit to an impossible, unconquerable world. I cannot defy my father, however, and continue to send the perpetual SOS. Finally, one Spanish magazine does a feature on Simon Taitz, "*orologico*" and the vanishing "*crocodilios.*"

Only then does Simon rest, for he had been shown the respect he had deserved from a time so long past it had preceded my existence.

I remember once being chased through the house and slapped for not greeting him at the door when he came home late at night. And then apologizing, weeping, until he forgave me, usually after a silence of several days.

I remember the last time I had tried to defy him. I had come home from camp happy, tanned, proud of myself. The word *camp* had transformed itself from my parents' connotation ("when I almost died in the camp") or from the oddball Camp Betar, to a communal joy-pot of adolescent fun amid the green smells of nature, so foreign to me in my urban veal box. I had worn some boy's "ID bracelet," a heavy chain-link encircling my slender wrist, the engraved name of my suitor falling casually down my hand. These IDs were status symbols among us girls, and wearing one had made me feel proud and female.

Whenever I arrived back from eight weeks of summer to our small apartment in the gray bleak Heights, I'd be sad for about a week, missing the freedoms and smells of youth and pleasure, reacclimatizing myself to the claustrophobia, the incessant demands, and the suppressed rage.

And sometimes, not suppressed.

Looking back, it was foolish to say what I said. But I never stopped trying to communicate with both my parents, bring them along on my developmental trips, share my growing acculturation. And the ID bracelet, a sign of my being a real American teenager now, had given me new courage.

"Daddy," I said, "when I was at camp I learned something new. I learned that I'm really too old for you to hit me now."

There was, perhaps, a second of silence, and then— WHAM!

He thumped me a good one. As with all other episodes of his literally heavy-handed rage, I fell to the floor, *thwack*, like a bug shot dead by a spray of Raid.

My father continued hitting me as I stayed there, half

crumpled, guarding my face, with which I'd done much sweet kissing over the summer. He never stopped, even when I got the lesson. Actually, I could never fully get his lessons in ultimate submission. He stopped only when his wrath had fully abated, his forty days of torrents to drown out the world. Finally, I lay on the floor and he was finished. I could hear my mother's ineffectual weeping, noticing that, unlike the times when my brother was hit, she had not screamed out for my father to stop. But although she was not crying hard, she was crying more than I was.

I was not crying this time. This time, I realized, I would write about my experience.

I went to my room, ripped a piece of paper out of a small, spine-coiled notebook, and wrote the words:

"I hate you, you fascist piece of *chara*." *Chara* was a daring curse word, all things considered. It was the Arab word for "shit."

I took the paper in my hand and slowly walked to our bathroom. Piece by piece, I ripped my midget-opus, ceremoniously freeing my passions to the acceptance of the sea, its conduit our toilet. Like openmouthed communion, the oval of water accepted my offering. My body, my blood, my passions.

And though the words reached no living heart then, they do now, and I can add to them: "But at the same time, Daddy, I love you. If only words could take your pain away, as sometimes they do mine."

In the end, of course, my father lost his store in Lincoln Center. The big, neon script banner, "Taitz" in pink, "Jewelers" in turquoise, was extinguished, the cooling wires lowered to the ground. But, just as inevitably, he didn't give up. After a short time, Simon and my mother found and rented a jeweler's "booth" in the National Jewelry Exchange on Forty-seventh Street, commonly known as the Diamond District. These booths consisted of little counters, scarcely separated, behind which diamond cutters, setters, and polishers, wholesale gemologists, gold engravers, and other jewelry specialists noisily plied their trade. My father was one of the few master watchmakers; he was nearly lost in that bustling exchange.

Simon brought his workbench and tools; Gita brought her velveteen trays of pearls and engagement solitaires. He nailed his precious OMEGA sign to the wall behind him, as well as a functional black laminate square with white letters spelling out "Taitz Jewelers," and they started up again.

The Jewelry Exchange was really a block-long avenue of old-world Jews, many of them Hasidic survivors of the Holocaust. While immigrants themselves, and traditional in their religious practice, my parents were not Hasidim, most of whom had come from Poland and Hungary. The Lithuanian strand of Jewry had always been more geared toward learning and rationality; there was no special costume of black frock coat and trousers, no earlocks, no beards, no rebbe to whom one came to ask all questions of life. There was intellectual independence and more than a touch of practical modernity. Furthermore, the Yiddish voices that surrounded my parents at the Jewelry Exchange were accented differently from their own classic version. It was like listening to English spoken in a thick Southern accent.

Unlike my father's little store, moreover, this open arcade was vast and cacophonous. Thousands of showcases glittered as you entered the building, a dizzying kaleidoscope. Fluorescent lights from both under and over the counters highlighted the diamonds, magnifying them into a glacial, dazzling world of snow-white. At the same time, the sound of thousands of voices, selling, buying, questioning, and bargaining, was an assault on the ears. Hands gestured, and hands were shaken; golden necklaces were draped on an endless chain of customers, reflected in hundreds of gleaming mirrors.

My parents' booth was all the way in the back, on the right-hand wall. Tucked in there, I felt they were safe from the sensual assault of this crazy crystal palace. But at first, my father hated everything about the exchange, even his place in it.

"It's a madhouse here; I can't make myself think!"

"But at least you have your spot here in the back, where it's a little quieter," I'd say on my visits to New York, trying to console him.

"But no one can find me here! They come in for a big ruby, or maybe a pin, or maybe just to have a good time and haggle and waste someone's time. But they're not coming in here for pocket watches. They look me over and pass by—there are so many choices, so much to catch their eyes."

After a while, however, my father again began to re-establish his name as a master watchmaker. Not only did his customers from the old neighborhood find him, but soon, more and more clients began to visit from all over the world. Word-of-mouth among collectors of rare timepieces began to make Simon a central stop again. He bought, sold, and fixed, growing more and more happy and prosperous. In the evening, he stored his treasures in the impenetrable vault downstairs, behind remarkably thick leaden bank doors.

My mother was happy, too. Right above that corner spot in the exchange was a little diner. Every day, she ran up and down the stairs, grabbing a danish for herself, a hot coffee for her husband. Apart from our long-abandoned trips to the delicatessen after movies, Gita had rarely had the chance to "go out to a restaurant." The Diamond Dairy Kosher Lunchnet was a small escape for her. It overlooked the floor of the exchange, so that even when you sat there, sharing a cheese or cherry blintz with your daughter, Sonia, who was visiting all the way from England, you could see all your friends and coworkers below. And they could see you. You could wave to each other and not feel alone.

The Jewess at Last

IT IS PRE-CHRISTMAS DINNERTIME in the great, drafty, wood-paneled College Hall, held a week before the holiday. At the long oak refectory table, I sit next to Mr. Simopoulos, a brilliantly eccentric philosophy don. Leaning over me, he intones into my ear:

"The world is made up of three kinds of people: Jews, honorary Jews, and SHITS!"

Paul is sitting across the table from us. He is one of Simopoulos's favorite students. We both burst out laughing, and Simop joins us.

"So, which are you?" I ask him.

"Jew and Honorary Jew, of course, you imbecile!"

Well, both seem to be in the minority here in England. Over the term, Jewish students have slowly begun gathering in my dorm room. Their names are Anglicized: Fenton for Feinstein, Wayne for Weinberg. (They have the reverse problem to what I suffered with *kashering* the name Brendan O'Neill.) They seem frightened even to "admit" that their name was once Cohen (the name of the priestly caste) and is now Cowan. It is only when they know that I, too, am Jewish—and more surprisingly, open about it, proud of it, even—that they come in, relax, and talk about their names, their beliefs, their wariness.

So this is the country that forms the spine of "European culture," the country of manners and containment. The people who like me tend to be the outsiders, the artists and actors, the weirdos and the rebellious aristocrats, out for a bit of real life. The Irish, the Scots, the Jews, and the Welsh; the black and the Arab—we bond. Benazir Bhutto is there, super cool in her purple kid-skin boots. People like her are called "Pakis" at Oxford. Most students feel no shame in their intolerance. After all, as the saying goes, "The wogs start at Calais."

On the contrary, it is expected that I be ashamed to be Jewish.

When I ask, innocently, if someone is Jewish, a non-Jewish student responds, "I don't know—I wouldn't *dream* of asking him." But why not? I am asking if that person is a descendant of Abraham, Moses, and David—not if they have a communicable sexual disease.

Paul's own parents can hardly look at me, so horrified that this dark-haired, sultry foreigner has got her claws into their firstborn son. He has taken me to his home in Stoke Poges, a small, prosperous town near Windsor Castle. The house, like the Queen's, or nearby Eton College, is built of stone. It being Sunday, we have roast beef and Yorkshire pudding, along with minted peas. Dessert is trifle and "blackberry fool."

Perhaps they just need to get to know me better. They need to know what a good, nice, smart girl I am, how hard I work, how much I try. I try to impress them. Stupidly, I don't realize that showing off is wrong in this culture—so I brag nonstop about all my accomplishments, the ones that make my father proud. I am actually hoping that they will like me for being a good student.

"And—what else? I—I was a valedictorian in high school. The Hebrew valedictorian. I actually gave my speech in modern Hebrew."

They are numb with disdain. Who talks of Hebrew, of all the—? Who brags of language skills? What is she getting at?

"My parents are Holocaust survivors," I tell them, falling fully into the shite pile. "They lost everything they owned, but did everything they could to give me a good education. Which no one could take from me. I'm actually on leave from Yale Law School."

I'm giving them the old one-two. First, the Holocaust—look how much we have suffered, how noble we are, how innocent and brave. And then, despite all that, Yale! Can you beat the Jews? Their phoenix-like rebirthing abilities? Their Helen Keller gumption? But they do not applaud, and I cannot feel their love with my feet, my ears, or any other part of me.

Their expression tells me that I have badly overestimated my accomplishments. They seem to be saying, to themselves (I am not worth telling):

"Our ancestors, toothless and on a farm holding a pitchfork of hay, would be better than yours with a golden mortarboard discovering the cure for cancer. We are English, born on English land. We don't *need* to wander about annoying people. We worship God in the Church of England, founded by an English King. Our prayers are all in good, proper English, the language of God, a civilized gentleman with more manners than your clan of sweaty parvenus have ever had."

"Better a Negress than a Jewess," his mother confides tearfully to Paul. When he tells me this, the words give me a complex frisson. Are such words and concepts really still in use?

Isabelle wears a fine golden cross on her neck. In her childhood village church, they told her that Jews are damned, that they killed Christ—a man who didn't brag and wasn't pushy about his Phi Beta Kappa key—and that we will therefore be cursed forever, not just on earth, where we must wander (and will again, if they can just get rid of Israel), but also in the afterlife. All she's done is take in what she was told, which is what most people do—including, to some extent, my own parents.

Paul feels his mum has fallen for easy propaganda and dated hocus-pocus. While believing in God, he cannot believe in the Christ story anymore (other than the good man's existence). He tells me that he has "envious aspirations" toward the simpler monotheism held by the Jews. He cites the Bible, particularly one passage in Genesis:

"'Numerous as the stars,' eh? I'd actually say 'brilliant as the stars.' He did make you that. And if you're an example, I'm hungry for more."

On the other hand, a good friend of his (who belongs to the Christian Union) comments as I pass: "Oh, here's Brother Abraham!" He gestures around his nose to indicate its prominence. With the other hand, he mimes holding a coin and rubbing it. He's not alone. On the TV in the college common room, the sitcoms joke about the Jews and their aversion to pork. We're not the only target. They make fun of all accents: the Spanish, the Italian, the Chinese. When I hear someone "do" an Eastern European accent, I want to say, That's my mother and my father and their friends! That's a bunch of refugees you're mocking, with accents born of exile. That accent will vanish with them. Why are you laughing? Do you even *speak* another language, the way they do?

And yet, I rarely go home to see my parents. I rarely hear their accents on the phone. Instead, we mostly correspond by mail. I write long, dreamy letters about the rain and the swans. I am sure I baffle them. Our lives together have never been about dreams, rain, and swans. I am sure I wrong them by being so far away. All my life they have been like my children, and now I am living my own life, a life that they would find somewhat mad. Why chase arguments, feuds, and old shadows?

Still, though I do not fly home often, they are on my mind daily. When I write to them, I address them, as always, as my *kindees*—an invented word, a nickname, based on *kinderlach*. I have been using this word more and more. These people are my children, my dependents, yet all I seem to do is willfully try to relive the worst parts of their lives, a would-be Jew in Europe. The "Brother Abraham" comments actually please me. They make a reality out of the nightmares I had heard all my life. I can confront them now.

Paul's father, Rikki (an old Boy Scout/Kipling nickname he favors), goads me now and then. He loves how angry and pointed I get about these little slights, how I get wound up like a desperate, talking doll. He is proud of being a white Anglo Saxon Protestant, better than anyone no matter what I say about his cultural myopia. Eventually, I come up with a parallel that nags at him. It's kind of an SAT analogy.

"England is to America as Judaism is to Christianity."

"So, you'd equate England and—and Judaism?"

"Yes," I say. "England is the root of the English-speaking empire which, you would agree, has popularized and cheapened its original quality. Look at American culture," I bait him.

"That's true. It's god-awful."

"So that's how you could see Judaism vis-à-vis Christianity. One is small and old-fashioned and riddled with rules and customs, and the other far more popular, with a simpler message and more universal appeal."

"Well," he says, "doesn't 'universal appeal' tell you something? There must be something to it if everyone believes in it. That's why, despite the occasional whisper of doubt, I'm a Christian—sheer numbers can't be wrong."

"Well, according to your logic, McDonald's is better than a three-star Michelin restaurant. More people eat at McDonald's."

"Oh, be quiet," he says grumpily, ruffling my hair. Rikki actually likes me far more than his wife does. He has traveled the world as a computer executive, but she has never knowingly met a Jew before.

Within a year, after I've received my MPhil in English literature, Paul cuts me off. He ceases all contact and exiles me from his world. His parents, who live not far away from Oxford, have told him that I have seduced him, body and mind, that I have hypnotized him. They have repeatedly motored up to Oxford to insist that he stop this crazy romance of his. Paul is only twenty-two years old now, and he must have been listening to them for months. When he does act he acts quickly, as though afraid of me and my tenacity. He is right to be afraid. I am not good at taking no for an answer. They are *all* right about me. I am a tenacious Jewess, a Scheherazade who will never run out of stories.

"Don't do this," I plead. More than anything, I never thought this particular story would end in fierce rejection.

He was supposed to choose me, to cross over the divide that separated us. He was supposed to love me even (or especially) when his parents didn't.

"She is sucking the life out of you" is the phrase they used, menace in their words matching the menace they see in me. I am a witch and a sorceress. He is the blond child whose blood is being taken by a succubus.

"She is toying with you. You're not the first, and you won't be the last." I am three years older than he, and I have had more experience, romantic and academic. Why should he rest his vulnerable heart on my loyalty? One could easily see their point of view. I have left my parents behind; I've left every trace of my life behind me. What kind of person could I be to do that?

Back home at 100 Overlook Terrace, I am now twenty-five years old and beaten. I didn't belong in law school and I didn't belong in England. In time, a battered green trunk, emblematic of my failure, arrives from Oxford. Packed by Paul, it is full of everything that we have shared together—fond notes, programs from plays I'd written there (one in which he'd starred), a letter from Lord Bullock awarding me a prize for short stories, one suede boot with a broken-off heel, an old Hebrew prayer book, my Wordsworth and my Dickens.

The nightmare has come true—I have been kicked out of Europe. And here in New York, I have few prospects. Now that I've gotten a graduate degree in English, I am considered overqualified for most entry-level jobs, including one at a publishing house, which involves fast and accurate typing. So I decide to go back to law school to finish my degree.

I am afraid to "just sit home and write." My parents are dubious about the arts, and the real possibility of failure would bring me back to where I started—a nothing, a flotsam, the refugees' kid. At least Yale Law is special. And at least my father is proud again.

Dan Greenleaf, Esquire

IN THAT SECOND YEAR of law school, the year of my return, I meet Dan Greenleaf, who is in his third and final year. Dan is the perfect rebound man for me, and ideal for my parents as well. After Jacob, they have waited more than five years for a Jewish man to ask for my hand in marriage. Dan is not only Jewish—his father is an oral surgeon in Brookline, Massachusetts. Prosperous and stylish, Dan rents a rambling beach house off campus, to which he drives in an ancient, lumpy Volvo. His clothes are like costumes—baggy pants and suspenders. Prematurely salt-and-peppered, Dan looks like Richard Gere in *American Gigolo* if, instead of a paid escort, Gere were playing a bookish Yale Law student in horn-rimmed glasses. His mother was an opera singer. His aunt produces documentaries. Not only is my Mr. Greenleaf at Yale Law, but he also graduated summa from Harvard College.

Dan shares his big funky house with actors and directors from the drama school. Chez Greenleaf, jazz plays through the sound system, actors roller-skate around, and clumps of interesting graduate students prepare African dishes requiring orange-colored spices, which we eat on vintage, mismatched dishes. Dinner conversation is witty, erudite, literary, political, pop-cultural.

As Dan would put it, "What's not to like?"

And he is right. This guy is not just a lawyer. He is a very nice Jewish boy, the sort my heart needs to rest on, like a parakeet on a perch or index finger. Though of a far more biting intellect than Jake's, Dan strokes my ruffled feathers, tells me to relax, fixes me a mean cocktail (he knows them all). One day, when it is cold outside and the New England wind is blowing, Dan buttons up my overcoat, just like in a '40s song. Another day he whispers into my ear the phrase I most need to hear:

"Baby, now you're safe."

It was a short trajectory. Before Dan, I wanted to risk myself, try my powers. I wanted to be unsafe so I could prove myself a peer to my parents' heroism and survival skills. But England has thrown me upside down and on my fragile head. I have indeed inhabited the sense of being the wandering and unwanted Jew. I crave the warmth and security that Dan Greenleaf offers. I like that he makes good challah French toast, delivered on a tray with Kenyan coffee. I like that he calls me *bubbeleh*, like an old Jewish man from the Borscht Belt.

"*Bubbeleh*—you're O-kay!"

Because of this "okay" feeling (which Jacob had offered me years ago, and I had arrogantly rejected), I quickly agree to marry Dan. Once the big rock is on my finger, the wedding caravan takes off with even more surprising velocity. We get a hall, a dress, a tux, pick a smorgasbord and plan a flower-bedecked chuppah. It seems no time at all before I am surrounded by hundreds of guests and two rabbis who tell me to walk around Dan seven times, as is the Jewish custom. I suddenly refuse. It is my only sign of rebellion, stemming not only from my sense of feminine pride but the fear that I should not be getting married at all.

People with broken hearts and bruised heads from being tossed upside down should probably not get married.

A few weeks before the wedding, I had told my father that I felt I was making a big mistake. I wasn't sure if it was Dan, specifically, that I wanted, or simply the healing sense of rescue he gave me. My father offered the following strange advice:

"Don't go backward. Always go forward."

This might well have been the secret of the brave, productive, and heroic life of Simon Taitz. And functional clocks do not go counterclockwise. But this is not good advice if you are heading for a cliff. (I realize this years later, with characteristic esprit de l'escalier.)

So we marry. In no time, Dan and I are surrounded by hundreds of gifts (espresso makers, enormous vases) and comfortably living in a floor-through in a townhouse in Greenwich Village. As Dan said, "What's not to like?" I am comfortable, and, true to his word, I am safe. As my father always dreamed, I am financially and socially sound: Dan and I are elite Manhattanites in the yuppie heyday of the 1980s. During the day, I work in litigation on the thirty-ninth floor of a law firm so prestigious that jaws drop when I mention it. The clients are all multinational corporations who pay hundred of dollars for each billable hour. We swat our opponents with yellow pads full of legalese (which I help write each and every day, often past midnight). We go to court in phalanxes, dozens of associates to each litigating warrior-partner.

Dan clerks for a federal judge. Along with the challah French toast, he sustains me with fresh baguettes and frothy cappuccini, and there are weekly flower arrangements that appear at the townhouse door. Still, I find my mind wandering to Paul. Maybe I don't like the feeling of being thrown away. Maybe I want to win another shot at the proverbial Ahasuerus beauty contest. Maybe I remember more passion in my past. Like most husbands, Dan becomes consumed by his work over time, and his attention to me begins to drift. Over the next few years, Dan's career rises meteorically. He leaves the house before I wake up and returns when I am asleep. Our bond wanes even as our possessions and bank accounts grow. I slowly regret joining my life to this man, whom I barely know.

What joined us was law school. Perhaps I could have resisted my wedding plans more forcefully had the date not been just weeks after graduation. It was all forward-moving continuum, like the mechanized walkways at a large airport. The question was never where are you going, but how fast can you get there. I was twenty-seven now, no "spring chicken." My parents were tired of waiting for me to do them proud. I was getting the Jewish husband (which made Gita happy) and the Juris Doctor degree (thrilling Simon), with them and for them.

My parents stand, small and modest, in the faux-medieval courtyard outside my dorm. It is only a short time before their daughter's name will be read by a stentorious voice, declaring her among the chosen few graduating Yale Law School. SONIA (named for his dead mother). JUDITH (a double-naming, for her brothers Jacob and Israel). TAITZ. Mr. and Mrs. Taitz, survivors, will now have a child who will speak for them, petition for them, write the letter to avert the next pogrom.

Resplendent in my cap and gown, puffed full of great job offers and the general air of privilege that is Yale, I notice how old and fragile they look. How did this happen? My father always looked a bit gray, but even my mother seems less rosy, and her shoes look clunky, almost orthopedic. Did they age while I was away from them at Oxford? Did my being so far away hurt them? Had I come home enough during the last years of law school? How had I let my *kindees* down like this?

Robert Sargent Shriver III is there, a warm and witty Kennedy scion known to all as Bobby, with whom I have developed a sweet friendship. He calls me "champ," and I love his boyish kindness. His sister Maria, not yet a TV correspondent, holds a movie camera, filming her brother and the surrounding scene of graduates and their parents. I can hear her narrating, her voice bright, amused and energetic. Bobby's parents are there, President Kennedy's remarkable sister Eunice, and Robert Sargent Shriver Jr., founder of the Peace Corps. All the other parents, not just the Shrivers, seem to have smooth hair. The women seem blonde, with hairbands, the men, white-haired and tall.

"*Sonialeh!*"

The word is trilled in three high notes. I turn to see my mother approaching, offering me a battered brown banana in crinkly, used tinfoil. She sweetly waves her linen hanky, which is embroidered with pansies. This is the sort of handkerchief she would wet with her own spit, holding my chin to wipe dirt off me during my childhood.

"Sonialeh! Do you want a good nice banana? Take a piece!"

She actually says this in Yiddish:

"Vilst du a gute shayne banan? Nem a shtick!"

"Not right now," I say, wondering if Maria Shriver is film-ing this. Hopefully, she will think that my mother is saying something intellectual and appropriate to the occasion. What does she know from Yiddish? Words like *nem a shtick* could never have emerged from the mouths of Sarge and Eunice.

My father wears his gray straw hat with the feather, the kind he always wore to visit me up at camp. He is so proud of me today; his carriage is straight as a soldier's.

"Smile, Sonialeh," says my mother, and she snaps a pic-ture of me.

The photo, which I see later, reveals my feelings: though of course smiling, I am constricted, ashamed of my own par-ents. I also feel guilty at being annoyed with the good peo-ple who gave me all my opportunities. Whose own schooling was cut short. Who slaved for me. I am not merely ambiva-lent. I am multivalent.

At least I have done right by them and graduated. They are proud of their daughter, wearing not only the law school mortarboard and gown (embellished with royal purple), but a sapphire and diamond engagement ring. They are thrilled that she is finally going to marry a Jewish guy, a law graduate, too, from a good family. Dan's parents do not find mine odd, or different. They know other Holocaust survi-vors; their own parents came over from Poland and Russia. They have heard the accents before.

Even the graduation speaker is a Holocaust survivor—it is Elie Wiesel, who survived the war as a teenager and wrote about it in unforgettable prose in books like *Night* and *The Gates of the Forest*. This man will ultimately win a Nobel Peace Prize, but that day I hear someone mocking his name on the program, pronouncing it "Weasel."

"Elly Weasel? Is that like Elly Clampett married Pop Goes the Weasel?"

He actually laughs, this graduate who happens to be a Jew from a prominent, though assimilated, Washingtonian family. I want to hit him on the head with my mortarboard, and I want Maria to get it on tape.

It is in this crappy, defeated, and pugnacious mood that I marry Dan Greenleaf.

THERE HAD BEEN ONE MORE defeat before the wedding. Several months before, I had written to Paul, telling him of my engagement. I confessed to him that I was not really certain about the marriage—that I didn't love Dan the way I loved him, that (despite the stew recipes from Mali) Dan did not have the passion, the wildness, the freedom in him that Paul had. This letter was, to mix Catholic metaphors with a Protestant paramour and a Jewish fiancé, a Hail Mary pass. I'd wanted Paul to stop the wedding. I'd wanted him to step forth, as though on the stage, and bellow: No! You can't! Think of our love! You can't marry this man, albeit Jewish and a Harvard/Yale grad, just to please your parents!

My letter to Paul is the tapping of a convict in a cell. *Here under duress. Please come and rescue.* Paul does not write back. I try to remember only the good of him, the part that loved me, not the one that threw my things out of the window of Staircase 7. What had his parents actually said to him? "What is she doing with you? A Jew? From New York? What is she playing at?"

My mother had asked me the same questions. "A goy?

From England? Don't you know he will one day get very drunk and maybe beat you?"

In the summer between my two years at Oxford, I had come to see my parents in Jerusalem, where they were vacationing. We sat on a balcony in the evening, enjoying hot tea and cool breezes. Beyond us lay a vista of white stones and evergreens, palm trees and golden domes. It was paradise; it felt like love and peace and reconciliation. And in that spirit, I tried to tell them about my new friend Paul, whose connection to me seemed to negate that rigid "vow" of only a few years ago.

"I have met someone totally wonderful."

"Oh?" My mother perks up, excited. Having not married my normal college boyfriend, the adorable and Jewish Jacob, I am rarely the source of *nachas* for her. She has nothing to say to her friends, whose own daughters are not only marrying but having children. When they ask about me, she is silent. Yale Law and Oxford mean nothing to her. If she had built me up from scratch, she would have had a daughter who taught school for a few years (lower grades), then had a few children for Bubbe (now it would be her, Gita) to feed and kiss and squeeze. But this daughter of hers went her own way, like a real crazy.

"I think this man is one of the special people on the earth," I say, more to my father than her. "Special" is one of his words, not hers.

"The ones who make the earth a better place, who sustain its goodness, who tip the balance." There is a Jewish legend about the Lamed-Vavniks—the Thirty-Six—meaning that at any given time, there are thirty-six saintly people alive and among us, in recognition of whom God refrains from destroying the world, even at its worst moments.

You don't have to be Jewish to be a Lamed-Vavnik. In

fact, the legend is that none of them are. These are the people who saved the Jews. These are the people who can feel other people's pain, their hearts are that big.

My mother, astute, smiles thinly. For all her usual cuddliness, she can be harsh and dry when the boundaries of her familiarity are crossed. She is like God in the garden: You have so many good fruits, why do you need this apple? Just to make trouble?

"So you met what, a *shaygetz*?" she spits out, decoding expertly. This word, unlike *goy*, is deadly pejorative. She pushes her glass of tea away and looks angrily over the hills of this enchanted city. Her eyes are narrow, hurt. From *shkutzim* (the plural) comes only pain. From *shkutzim* she has had only grief—a dead father, dead brothers, neighbors rounding them up in the middle of the night. Many wearing crosses and feeling good about the Christ-killers in a forced march out of town. She will never, ever go back to Lithuania. For her, at bitter times, all people and places can transform into Lithuania. Even I, her daughter, can be Lithuania. She would not be surprised.

"Well, he's not exactly Jewish right now, but he is good, and kind, and—"

"Yeh. Sure. So good and kind. Romantic, like Clark Gable."

I'm surprised by the movie-magazine reference. Not that it is fanciful and out of place. No, the opposite. For me, those people and their stories have always been real. Ricky is real, and Lucy is real, and Elizabeth's magical eyes? Nothing truer. Surely, Doris Day was real to my mother. Doesn't she realize that most of these people were—are—goyim, *shkutzim*? Has she really never taken our folk legends seriously? I have. The legends taught me that anyone is accessible. Even an English actor, handsome as Henry Fonda, dressed as Don Juan, can descend from the stage and see you one day.

I turn to my father, who has always had his poetic side.

"Didn't you ever meet someone who was surprisingly wonderful—so much so that you questioned everything?"

"I know what you are talking about," he says, kindly not bringing up the vow I made to stay close to Judaism, and not in this new, contrived way of the special goy who loves me and my people.

"Here, in Jerusalem," he continues, "I sometimes talk to the priests and ministers. I see them everywhere. They have great souls, many of them. I tell them of my life in the camps, and how I believed in God, and they understand me. And I understand them, too. I think of them as my friends here.

"And yet," he goes on, "there are only thirty-six Lamed-Vavniks. And the world has almost six billion people in it. It is possible that you met one, but not so likely."

"But what about the Nazi you talked about—the nice one?"

"You mean the one who—?"

"Yes, tell me that story again," I say to my father. "I want to hear it again."

"I heard it enough times," says my mother, but she takes up her tea glass again and sips from it. She seems cheered as my father tells his tale.

My father had met someone special from the hidden world of goodness back in the concentration camp. He had brought out the kindness in him, so that it showed to all the Jews in his watch shop.

It was Passover time, and of course there would be no matzohs—the unleavened bread that Jews are commanded to eat for eight days, to remind them of their years of slavery in Egypt. They had left in an exodus so swift that their bread had not had time to rise. My father had tried to keep his faith during his time in Dachau. As Passover approached, he began brooding about matzoh.

One of the Nazi officers liked him, he told me. One of them admired his workmanship, his watches. He had liked the little touch of hero in my father, his direct and honest ways. They could talk sometimes, my father said, as though one were not a dirty Jew and the other an evil murderer.

As Passover approached, my father worked up the nerve to talk about it to this Nazi. He approached him, and said:

"My mind is very troubled. I cannot work."

"You can't work? What do you mean, you can't work?"

"A man needs bread to work."

"Fine, yes, we give you bread."

Indeed, the Jews in the watchmaker's shop were fed fairly well for Dachau prisoners; with indoor shelter and peaceful labor (or the semblance of it, since most could not really fix watches), many kept their strength and survived the horrors, thanks to my father.

"Yes, you give us bread. But there is a time that we cannot eat it."

"What are you talking about?" The man was becoming irritated.

My father paused for moment, then asked:

"Do you believe in God?"

The Nazi thought for a minute, then answered, "Yes."

"Have you read the Five Books of Moses?"

"Well, so?"

"Well, I too believe in God, and in this Bible, God commands the Jews not to eat leavened bread on the days of Passover. In a few days, it will be Passover. And I am forbidden to disobey him.

"There is a special kind of bread that is allowed. It is called matzoh. This unleavened bread we can eat. In fact, we are commanded to eat it."

"Where do you think you are getting such bread here in Dachau?"

"It is very easy to bake. My father was a miller, and my mother used to take a little milled grain, add water, and bake it for no more than three minutes. No more, no less—that is how you make matzoh."

"And this is what you Jews eat every year?"

"Yes. This is a lasting commandment, and we must all follow it, whatever the circumstances."

The Nazi walked around the workshop. He looked at all the workers, bent over their watches, then returned to my father.

"How much would you need for your people here?"

"Not much—we really only have to eat an 'olive-size' piece each day. But more would of course be better."

"I will talk to my wife about this."

And with that, the Nazi turned and left.

When Passover came, the man returned with a large box of crudely made flatbreads. He also took several glass jars out of a net bag.

"These are preserves, which my wife makes. She thought her matzoh looks so dry, maybe you would need something else with it. You will eat strawberry? I think it is her best."

My life has been inspired by that story, in particular the way my father found an angel inside the devil. It is what I was looking for in Brendan, the Irish seducer of Columbia University, and in Paul, the angel of Oxford who once turned his shining countenance on me. Sometimes these angels are dangerous to look for, hard to keep. But I need to keep trying.

Lovely, Dark and Deep

ONE DAY, I toss everything away on one phone call, made while staring at the flower arrangement on my majestic law-firm desk. The fragrance of lilies and roses has made me think of weddings, of my wedding, and why I did not end up marrying Paul.

Paul picks up my transatlantic SOS and the first thing he does is shout: "Why didn't you answer my letters?"

He sounds like he is in the same room, he is shouting so loudly.

"You wrote a letter? To me?"

"More than one, you imbecile. You told me you were going to get married, so of *course* I kept writing to you, over and over."

My mother must have hidden his letters from me. Or tossed them out.

My mother must know that she has tossed out love letters from Paul. She must have known this for years and never mentioned it. But I have no time to dwell on this betrayal. In her mind, Gita was saving me from danger (putting me back on my playground leash so the *vilde chayes* did not hurt me), and in any case, Paul is now, this minute, sort of proposing.

"Not marrying you myself was the worst thing I've ever done," he says. "You are the only person like you in the world, and everyone here bores me stupid."

Please repeat?

He does.

In no time at all, like a crazy, I am on my way back to England. Running, as my mother did, back to the one she loved. Redeemed, relieved, restored.

My mother, of course, is in shock. I am leaving my husband? My job? My long-awaited normalcy? Dan and I have been married for several years. If I had an announcement to make, it should have been about a grandchild for her, not this step back into the *meshuggeneh* times.

My father wants to take my side, but it's harder and harder to do.

"For this—this Paul"—the name sounds truly odd in his mouth—"you would leave your life here with a good, hard-working man, a Harvard-Yale graduate, a lawyer?" He knew me too well to think I was happy with my legal career and its grinding, militaristic routines. But what of the fact that I was married to a man with a life of accomplishment?

"I always loved Paul," I say. "I married Dan out of fear and sorrow, and to make you happy. But I was never really happy with him. We were like brother and sister, a pair of worn old shoes. We didn't dance."

This last piece of information alarms them both. After all, they had met at the Survivors' Ball; they had waltzed together to Strauss. For all their battles, my parents had always danced together and shared a physical bond.

"You didn't dance?" My mother cannot believe that I, whom she has grown to approvingly consider a real "hotsy-totsy," would marry a mild man like that.

"He doesn't like to—to dance with me. And even when we try to dance," I add, the true metaphor reappearing, "it's very boring. For both of us."

"That's not good," my mother acknowledges, shaking her head.

We are all back in my childhood kitchen, eating bagels and farmer cheese and jam, and drinking tea. My father, as he always does at the table, is wearing a yarmulka.

"And what about your Jewishness? What will happen should you eventually marry this English man?"

"I will always be Jewish," I say. "I promised you that before I left for England. I hope, someday soon, that Paul will convert. He has indicated that Judaism draws him."

My mother wants to interrupt, but I speak quickly and forcefully: "No matter what, my children will be Jewish, as the Jewish law itself says. If the mother is Jewish, the children are Jewish, too. I will raise them to know who they are and who you are and who I am."

It is to my parents' eternal credit that when they waved goodbye to me at the airport there were tears of hope in their eyes.

The final step of Paul's conversion is a *mikvah*, a ritual pool of sunlit fresh water in which he floats like a fetus. He has been studying Judaism, its practice and philosophy, for a year, and his naked immersion is the final metamorphosis.

He also draws close to my parents. Their old-world simplicity both amuses and moves him. He loves their warmth, their desire to touch, to ask nosy questions.

During his time of Jewish study, Simon and Gita have grown to accept Paul like a son of their own; they shower him with hugs and plant money in his pockets. My father asks him regularly, as he has always asked me, "What did you accomplish today?" Paul is glad to be asked; in England, most fathers do not fawn on their sons or crave details of their life's minutiae. Nor are career and business always the first topic of conversation there. My father cannot get enough of this man, who listens, in return, to all his stories.

My father's interest in his future son-in-law is timely. His daughter is not what she used to be in the ambition department. With Paul in America, I have gone off the bullet-train rails a bit, writing articles and stories and plays, practicing law only in the most desultory fashion (part-time in a small, white-collar criminal firm), wondering about when to start a family. Paul, on the other hand, who has no end of talents (he is numerate and a good negotiator), has found a job at a big New York bank with a legendary, German Jewish name. He wears a nice suit and commands a good salary and bonus. This man is a mensch: he will be a provider, maybe even a philanthropist. He sits tall in the synagogue's men's section near my much smaller father, a tallis on his shoulders. He eats my mother's holiday food, the chopped liver and the kreplach, the kosher jello laden with canned fruit. Though his Hebrew is still rudimentary, he tries to sing along when my father says grace after our Sabbath meals. "Chana, bracha, lecha, kol," he attempts. He even calls me "Sonialeh." As in, when my mother asks him, "So, are you happy here in New York and being a Jew on Rosh Hashanah?"

He answers sweetly, "Of course, how could I not when I have my Sonialeh?"

Our small wedding takes place in the Ritz Carlton, on a winter's day, overlooking Central Park. Snow on the ground, snowflakes in the air, champagne, white roses, hansom cabs below us.

After the ceremony, my father takes Isabelle, his new in-law, aside.

"I feel that I must apologize to you," he says to Paul's mother.

"Whatever for?" she says, momentarily taken aback.

"I am so sorry that my happiness and joy come at your expense." He is talking about Paul's leaving her Christian faith and becoming a Jew. He is talking about my small victory over the past. In some way, I have stolen her son to shore up my people. In some way, I have fought an old, bloody battle (in my head, but perhaps also in hers) and won. But now, when people speak up against the Jews, my tall blond husband will stop them. He will say (with that English accent):

"Now see here. I myself happen to be a Jew. My wife and children are Jews. Stop that nonsense at once."

He actually does make a similar speech when, early in his career, a colleague (who soon also marries a dark-haired "Jewess") bangs and rocks a soda machine, yelling, "Stop jewing my money!" Paul has heard *jew* as a verb before, in England. In the past, he was silent, but now he knows what to do. From small words of hate, anything can happen. Did happen. One third of the Jewish people died in the Holocaust, along with gypsies, homosexuals, the disabled, and other insulted and despised minorities. But now, what was lost will be made right. The same year I remarry, Dan does, too. He and his wife will have three Jewish children. (Jacob also begets three Jewish children.) And Paul and I will have three Jewish children of our own.

Isabelle does not wear her cross to the wedding ceremony. She wears a kelly green suit with a stylish hat to match. On our turf, though beautiful and elegant as always, she is fractionally shaky, and Simon has the heart to reach out to her. He has been where she has been, a stranger in a new land. And so he apologizes to her.

But she answers, with shiny tears in her eyes:

"No, Simon. I am truly happy today. They are a beautiful couple, a prince and a princess, and they should have been together long ago."

She has had long talks with her vicar, who has reassured her that Jews are their spiritual ancestors. All will be well in this marriage, he has promised. Everyone in her village parish, Isabelle tells my father, has prayed for a successful journey for her and her husband, and that their meeting with my parents would be joyful. And it was. They share deep similarities—honesty, love of learning, lack of pretension—and faith.

The fact that my parents live in their small apartment and do not try to impress anyone—the very fact that they are not like their Riverdale friends (cigarette holders, scampi)—relaxes Paul's equally unpretentious parents. They like listening as my father talks simply of a familiar God, the one who saved Daniel from the lion's den, the one in the psalms, who comforts the hurt. They love my cute, pink-cheeked mother, who runs in and out of the kitchen, dewy with service, offering up tea with lemon and home-baked pound cake. Fears melt away from both sides of the divide.

"Oy," says my mother, finally sitting and lightly dunking her Swee-Touch-Nee teabag, "you are such nice people!"

And there is joy in her eyes, for the relief, for the tea, for the cake that goes with it.

"As are you," says Rikki.

Isabelle takes Simon's large hands in hers as she says, tears in her eyes, "We have so much in common." And he answers, "We share the same world and the same God above us. Your son is my son, and my daughter is your daughter."

After we are married, Isabelle and Rikki visit frequently, and each time they visit, they stop by Overlook Terrace for a Friday night meal with Simon and Gita, whom they have grown to love. The four of them share their own holy communion over bread and wine, as candles glow on a table set with white lacy cloth (covered, you should know, with plastic). My father sings, his voice deep and passionate, of the Sabbath peace. The mantel clock tolls the hours in Westminster chimes. The brass notes reverberate, are still. Time stops, hovers, with a sense of infinity

And so, we are all together. We travel, celebrate, share *simchas*, birthdays and holidays. We are joyful, we parents, children, and grandchildren, for the next ten years.

The Great Bully

IT MUST HAVE been especially hard for my father to actually have to die. He had survived so many near-deaths—not just the Nazis but the Communists just before them, not just the Germans but the Lithuanians alongside, and the Cossacks, before, who had murdered his father. On some level, amid all the bloodshed and violence, he must have felt oddly immortal.

Here, in America, where he became more and more devout year by year, he continued to put his faith in God, the Father who'd saved him, who would always be there. He had had the bravery to start life over, have a family, build a watch and jewelry business. And though he had been robbed a few times, he had done well overall. He felt safe in the world, contented with the fact that he had succeeded in sending both children to graduate school, not once, but twice (I with my law and MPhil degrees; my brother with law and business degrees). He even had a "nest egg" that he was saving up for us and our children. All of it was locked behind the impenetrable doors of the Jewelry Exchange vault.

And then, in his eightieth year, he was robbed again.

The safe, somehow, was blasted wide open and emptied of everything—the best of his pocket watches included. This was like losing a museum full of irreplaceable art. Like losing a village of people, or a family.

But all he said was, "I will start over again. I will find new watches and I will fix them and sell them." He was always determined to move forward. And in doing so, fate allowed him to do another great deed in his life.

One day, weeks after the robbery, a man came in with one of Simon's own stolen pocket watches. Unknowingly, he tried to sell it to the watchmaker himself, who knew its face as well as his own. Once she realized the man was a thief, my mother opened her mouth and screamed. Soon everyone began shouting out the verbal alarm of the Jewelry Exchange in the presence of danger.

"Chap zem!"

The words are Yiddish for "Catch them!" Immediately, all the corridors were blocked by fellow jewelers. Within minutes, the man with the stolen watches was caught. Surrounded by angry men, the thief was dragged back to my father's corner counter. Security guards ran over, guns drawn. A crowd gathered as Simon was asked what he wanted to do with this gonif, this thief.

The trapped man began to weep, begging in Yiddish. He told my father that if he was questioned by the authorities, whether he talked or not, he'd be a dead man on the street.

"Ich vil zein a gehargete mensch!!"

The thief pleaded: His fencing ring was large and vicious; he was only a pawn, one of many; he would be murdered for getting caught.

Simon let him go.

"I felt sorry for this unfortunate person," he said later

to his friends and colleagues. "I couldn't be responsible for his death. Nothing is worth that, not even the watches."

To the security guards, he said, in English, "I am not so sure that he was the bad man. I think I made a mistake."

Thus my father finds himself at eighty, still getting up at dawn and riding the subway downtown from 190th Street to Fifty-ninth, then transferring trains to get to Forty-seventh. Simon does not mind—work is all he knows—but intermittently, he complains about little aches and pains, particularly in his back.

And just as quickly, he dismisses them.

"I guess I'm not a youngster anymore."

When I was a little girl visiting my parents at the store, everyone used to think Simon was my grandfather.

"Aren't you good to help your grandpa out!"

The first time I heard this (I must have been seven or eight), I was shocked, but soon I got used to it. I even began making what I thought of as a witticism; I'd answer, "Oh, he's just like a father to me."

No one ever laughed at that. It occurs to me now that I'd implied that my real father was dead. He wasn't. He only looked as though he were a few months away from croaking. Simon's nearly bald head, the barrel-chest, the exaggerated, hyper-masculine features—all these turned him into an old man by the time of my birth—when he was only forty. Now, forty years later, he looks no worse to me, still natty in his starched white shirt and charcoal suit, with a tie that always had some trace of cherry-red in it. He loved red; to him it represented bravery and vigor, the very stuff of life.

Soon after, however, my father's final death sentence arrives. He is diagnosed with late-stage lung cancer, metastasized to the bone. The cancer is inoperable and incurable. Simon had never smoked. He must have gotten it after so many years of exposure to benzene, with which he wiped the inner workings of his timepieces. He had by now worked at his trade for more than sixty-five years.

When I used to tell him that benzene was a potent carcinogen, he'd laugh, and say: "I grew up with it. I used to wash my hands in it. I breathed it day and night." He had taken benzene into the bedroom with him, where he had a little workbench. He had even worked there on Sundays. My mother, I realized, had also been exposed.

Now, Simon visits a well-known oncologist. With hope in his eyes, he sees Hebrew writing on the wall, an expensively framed doctor's credo of the great biblical scholar and physician Maimonides. He feels reassured. The educated Jewish doctor will save him.

"Well, Dr. Highman," he says, jovially. "Can you help me out?"

The doctor takes his time answering. I immediately dislike him. It is a cold day in autumn. My parents are wearing coats, hats, scarves, and gloves. The doctor asks my father and mother to sit, but allows me to stand in the corner holding everything. He gives none of us eye contact. Instead, he stares into his computer screen, as though he could find an answer there. He plays with a rollerball mouse, rolling, rolling.

My father's question—"Can you help me out?"—reverberates in my heart.

He had often asked me that, when he wanted me to read something to him, explain a passage in the paper, or a word, or when he had asked me to "write a letter" for him, to a landlord, to the government, to a client.

And now, very patiently, he is asking for help.

God, he said, had always helped him. He repeated this every year, at Passover, reading with emphasis from the traditional Haggadah.

"In every generation, a man is obliged to see himself *as if he himself* came out of Egypt."

And, he'd say, "I do see myself that way. I *did* come out of Egypt."

And when he'd read the passage "up until now your tender mercies have helped us, and may you never desert us, forever," he'd stop, and savor the words. He seemed to believe that God could be counted on forever.

How could he, of all people, believe that?

Still, he did. Maybe the fact that he survived a death camp caused him to believe that he could survive anything.

In the doctor's office, as the specialist continues rolling his ball in what seems a desultory way, my father sits and waits for his verdict.

Finally, I fill the silence.

"Of *course* he can help you! There is always some way to help," I say pointedly. Like being kind enough to look a patient in the eye. Like not acting as though sickness and death were embarrassing, untoward. Why on earth did this constipated creep go into oncology?

Eventually, Dr. Highman looks up from his computer and says, blandly, "There are many treatments available. I could hardly list them all."

I can feel my father relax at the thought that the situation will be dealt with, with action. That it will be met, and wrestled with.

"I will take any treatment," he says, as though he were a volunteer. "Even if I lose my beautiful hair." Being bald, he often joked about "his beautiful hair."

The doctor doesn't smile. He stands up and, indicating that the meeting is over, walks past us to open the door and step outside to freedom.

"So there is hope?" my father persists, as the doctor races down the corridor. Turning his head around, he throws these words over his back: "My secretary will set you up with a schedule."

"Of course there is hope," I insist, handing out the coats, hats, scarves, and gloves. After all, we all believed not only in disasters, but in miracles. Furthermore, being overeducated, I know I will spend as long as it takes to get my father out of his death sentence. Surely there is something on the Internet.

Unfortunately, there is, and so I become an expert on incurable cancers and the many—surprisingly unknown—"cures" that are amazingly offered, at a high price. Some I remember include coffee enemas, special "greens," chemicals, crystals, vitamins, and muds. In one mad episode, I contact a "specialist" who sells the cartilage of goat tracheas, crushed into little pills, each costing about ten dollars.

To get my hands on these, I drive into the remote countryside and literally pass the "doctor's" Dobermans to get to his barn, I mean "laboratory." Grabbing the unlabeled bottles of goat gizzard, I run back to the car, tearing back to the city to give my father his cure. Just to make sure, I also begin ordering rare soups from the Orient, freeze-dried and containing an ambitious assortment of odd fungi. As if this were not enough (it isn't; the cancer spreads from lung, to bone, to brain), I buy an assortment of New Age tapes to help my poor father relax, as well as "realize" himself. He listens to them with puzzlement, putting one on pause to ask,

"Do I really have to listen to this *dreck*?"

I tell him that he does not.

In the midst of all this, my husband falls ill with an intestinal blockage requiring immediate, life-saving surgery. In the hospital, he nearly dies three times—once from the blockage itself, once from the fever of unknown origin that succeeds the massive, lengthy abdominal operation, and once from that fever invading his heart and nearly stopping it.

While Paul slowly recuperates, I tell my father about his ordeal. I want his concern, and I want him to feel as though his strength can still support me. Now that Paul is out of danger, I narrate everything that has been happening to him, me, and our three small children. Echoes of my namesake's early widowhood, with three young ones, have haunted me, and I am relieved we have survived this near-disaster.

My children had been scared when their father had first gone into the hospital. In order to reassure them, Paul and I made a movie on our video cam, one in which he smiled and said he was feeling much better and that his tummy was much better and his intestines were now capable of passing gas.

They loved that detail.

Then I shot a close-up of some horrible yellowish hospital pudding, and Paul, pinching his nose shut in the background, said, "Yech!! I have to eat ten bowls of this before they let me out."

Emma, Gabriel, and Phoebe had laughed at the challenge. Each day until Paul came home, they asked if he had "finished the pudding." It was a game to them, and they passed through this trauma unscathed. The last thing I would ever do, after the childhood I had had, was to frighten them unnecessarily, or burden them with possibilities they could not begin to fathom. But the truth was, my children (aged seven, five, and three) had almost lost their father.

"Paul almost died, Daddy," I say, over the phone. "I think he'll be okay now."

But my father, who will never recover, does not seem the least bit interested.

All he says is, "That is good," and then changes the subject to something in the news. A few hours later, he calls me back, and says:

"Please forgive me. I don't know why I spoke so strangely. Maybe I didn't hear somehow, or didn't understand what you said. Please send your husband, your wonderful husband, Paul, my love and my blessings."

Eventually, in perhaps a replay of my early childhood, Simon reverts to boundless fury. I recognize the sudden-cuckoo rage I saw when he was hitting my brother or belittling my mother, a rage that, over the years, had largely cooled down.

In the hospice we find for him, his madness is met by brusque impatience. When he threatens the staff and shouts, they give him large, unconscionable doses of Haldol, a potent antipsychotic. The pills are so toxic to his frail body that they knock him into a stupor. Ultimately, he develops tardive dyskinesia, an irreversible tremor in the limbs. My father's hands shake so that he cannot feed himself, and the staff, avoiding him, rarely steps into the room to see if he is fed. When I am there to watch him, I see that not only do his hands tremble but his face as well. I try to squeeze the juice of an orange into his mouth, but most of it lands on his hospital gown.

Hospice is meant for the dying only; my father's placement there means no more hospital and no more hope. His oncologist, after ravaging him with nonstop chemotherapy and radiation to the brain, is through with him. Simon will never see him again, nor any other vestige of his previous life. Friends and colleagues—people who used to travel the world to give him their rare watches for repair—all are reluctant to visit him in the final station of the terminally ill. My mother, who must work at closing their business, cannot handle the screams, not his and those of his fellow emaciated prisoners. Each visit to this hospice ravages her nervous system.

One day, as I reach my father's bedside, he grips my arm with ferocious strength and won't let go. Pulling me toward him, he tells me that during the night, a German forced him into leather restraints, both arms and legs, and yelled at him to behave and shut his mouth.

"Like a real fine Nazi," he says, his mouth tasting the sarcastic bitterness of each word. "This is worse here than any death camp."

I'm not sure whether his story is true or whether his brain tumor has grown exponentially. I check with the desk, and an apathetic administrator tells me that, yes, there often is a young, tall German man on duty at night.

"Oh, yeah," she acknowledges, chuckling. "Horst can be a little heavy-handed at times. But you know, these dying people, they go crazy at night, they get the terrors."

I ask her to make sure that my father will not see Horst again at any time, and that regardless of whom he sees, they will not tie him up like an animal. Returning to his room with a feeling of justice accomplished, I reassure my father that he will never have another such night—

"GET OUT!!"

My father blasts me, so suddenly and loudly, with such gleaming hatred in his eyes that I jump back.

He stares at me for a moment with contempt. It is like

looking into a night-guard's pitiless eyes. It is like falling down a bottomless black hole, and I don't even know that I am crying until he shouts again.

"YOUR TEARS DON'T MOVE ME!!"

I had always thought he could see deep within, to the beating heart at the center of a broken world. I had thought my father, repairer of watches, was privy to the secrets of the universe. But he is no longer the hero at the center of his story. He is back in a death camp and he knows it. And this humble lot of all mankind, this mortal terminus, is something he cannot understand or tolerate. He cannot move forward. He is stuck. He raves.

There is little more he can teach me.

On other visits, my dying father is soft and docile.

"Why do you even bother to visit me? You have a recovering husband, and small children to look after, too."

"It's a great honor to see you, Daddy."

"What?" he says, and I can see that he is pleased.

"Yes, an honor. I always wanted to spend more time with you, but you were working so hard. Everyone is fine now. Paul is better, the kids are in school. Where else would I want to be?"

He smiles, moved. His eyes are wet, as they are when he is touched by something beautiful. His tears move me.

Another day, he tells me that Paul and his parents have brought him the greatest happiness, and he thanks me for bringing them into his life.

"So I didn't break my vow?"

"Never. You have always been the most faithful Karaputzi. And your little family, your children, these wonderful people from England, they have all brought me such hope."

Please Send Help at Once

WHEN I WAS GROWING UP, my parents' store in Lincoln Center had had an emergency system whereby if you rattled the door or shook the windows a phone call would go out. This message would be relayed to the police station and also to our apartment, which meant me, alone after school.

> *A hold-up!*
> *Or robbery!*
> *Is taking place*
> *At Taitz Jewelers!*
> *Located at:*
> *1889 Broadway*
> *PLEASE SEND HELP AT ONCE!!*
> *PLEASE SEND HELP AT ONCE!!*

Horrified, I usually dropped the phone in panic whenever I got this message, and literally ran around the house, wondering what I should do. Despite the fact that these calls were, thankfully, only false alarms, each time they seemed real to me: *This is it.* Tragedies like this happened, I knew all too well. My parents were being held up, probably killed, and I could do nothing about it. The system would often be triggered as my parents locked up at night, so when I tried to call back, no one would answer. They would be on their way to the subway, and I would picture them dead of multiple gunshots. I would pace the house until they came home and relieved me of my terror, my guilt for not having saved them.

Saving my father from death was a familiar "must-do" on my list. After all, hadn't he suffered enough? Hadn't he faced that bully, death, enough times?

Most important, wasn't it my father's role in life to "survive," and mine, if necessary, to devote myself to saving him? Wasn't I his own private Wallenberg? This is why I had been born; this was my Queen Esther moment. This was what all the education had been for: this moment, this ultimate emergency. And now, I could rescue for all I was worth. I would find out what I was worth. A match with God himself. Just what my father, and perhaps I, had always been waiting for. Death as the ultimate bully, the inevitable Nazi.

On the other hand, this disease—as predicted by any reasonable prognosis of stage-four cancer—is indomitable. Day by day, my father looks thinner and more haggard. "Like a concentration camp victim," as the sadly accurate cliché goes. Even before his relegation to the hospice, his mind had been slipping horribly.

On one of his final chemotherapy appointments, he stands up, drops his pants, and bends over for the nurse to see. "Can you see where it hurts me inside?" Apart from the shock of this action (this was a most fastidious and dignified man), I see that his haunches, legs, thighs, and buttocks are gone. All that is left are the bones of his pelvis, skin hanging off.

Later, in a last effort, my father is given a series of radiation treatments, aimed at the center of his brow. The technician puts an indelible X there, in black, so that the spot can be found on multiple visits. Must this man wear the mark of Cain? What has he ever done to deserve this?

One day, my father, who has worked all his life, puts his head down on his special watchmaker's work table. This is something new, and awful, and it means that this fighter is beginning to wobble, to lose.

The Exchange is like a big village, a collective organism, and news spreads from booth to booth. I overhear my father's neighbor, an Israeli jeweler in the booth perpendicular to his, murmur, in Hebrew:

"Hineh sof shel adam." Here is the end of a man. What a horrible, biblical sound these words had; they have stayed in my mind until now. And it was true.

In his last days at the nightmarish hospice, as I feed him the orange that drips all over his gown, my father looks at me so sorrowfully that all I can think of saying is:

Min hametzar karati Yah
Anani bemerchav Yah

From the narrow strait I called out to God
God answered me with his freedom

I am quoting from his favorite psalm, recited on all the Jewish pilgrimage festivals. I am hinting that death can be a broad and freeing place. My father is trapped, and neither of us can stand the indignity of it. Death has never been spoken of before, not ever, but now it is his only hope of liberation. God will answer you with freedom, Daddy. You

deserve never to worry again about being trapped and hurt.
Silently, Simon's lips begin to mouth the words:

Shma Yisroel
Adonai Elohenu
Adonai Echad

These are the last words that are spoken by an observant
Jew. They were surely spoken by a million doomed voices in
the Holocaust he had survived. Forming those words, over
and over, my father, at last, was surrendering.

Real Lamed-Vavniks

AFTER A GREAT DEAL OF EFFORT, I find my father a bed in a better hospice outside Manhattan. Improbably, he is headed for Calvary Hospice, run by the Catholic diocese. How many times had my father railed against the Catholic Lithuanians who had helped the Nazis take over their country and send him to hell? How many times had I heard about his childhood Easter Sundays, dodging the congregants, freshly released from their Judas-laden sermons, itching to bash in a Jewish skull?

"Why do you deny it, Simon?" even his Catholic friends, little boys whom he skated with, with whom he threw chestnuts, would taunt. "You know you killed Christ. And you know that you make your Passover bread out of blood. The blood of Christian children. Admit it."

It was doubly ironic to me as a child, knowing that blood, even animal blood, was forbidden to Jews. "The blood is the soul," the Bible explains, using the Hebrew word *nefesh*—simultaneously elevating us and the world of the animals. There was a soul in the world of flesh. And there was no blood,

I knew, but lots of soul, in the matzoh the Nazi's wife had baked for my father and his fellow workshop men, in Dachau.

My father had said he smelled "Jewish blood" in the stones of the Spanish monastery in Washington Heights. The Cloisters were not, for him, a place of holy contemplation, but of trials and torture. There was a straight line, for him, between the Inquisition and the boys who shouted at him after Easter services, between those who killed his mother and those who watched, unmoved by mercy.

And yet, this merciful hospice is quintessentially Catholic, full of ministering women called Sisters. No place could be more full of grace in its treatment of the dying. The nuns, who remove a large crucifix from above Simon's bed, are as gentle as the mothers of newborns. I think about how Christ's skinny, twisted form is so like that of the dying, indeed so like the bodies of those who suffered and starved in the Holocaust, in all the global genocides that never seem to end. The nuns know suffering as I do—that makes them my spiritual sisters and mothers. Through them, I realize the full meaning of *gemilut chassadim*, the granting of mercies. These humble women are the real Lamed-Vavniks—the people whose modest goodness supports the world. They never give a ranting person Haldol, or tie him to a steel bed with thick, black hospital restraints. They sit with the poor soul, invigilating restlessness. Their silent goodness calms even my father, my wounded lion of Judah.

He rests.

In the end, the watchmaker's hands move slowly in the air above his body. It is a kind of survivor's last ballet: He lies in a coma, but his hands still open the magical gateways of pocket watches. On his last day of life, my father wakes up and looks into the round, pale face of Gita, his wife. Despite all the years of thankless work and insult, she bends over and kisses him, and he responds. He lowers his hardworking hands and puts them on her cheeks, which he covers with kisses. He does not want to let her go. It is as though he has seen her sweet and loyal face for the first time. But it is also the last time they will see each other on earth. My mother gives him one last hug and leaves the room hurriedly. Her face is wet with tears and with his kisses.

I follow her out. "I can't anymore," she says. "I can't watch him die. I'll go to the store and take care of the merchandise." She is referring to the watches and clocks, still coming in every day, but which will never be fixed. They will be returned to their owners, sent off to another watchmaker (the new ones come from India and South America) or sold at a loss.

Returning to my father, I sit and begin to understand why Gita had had to run from the hospital long ago when my tonsils were removed. She had seen too much suffering and death in her life to ever wait for more. Now my mother runs to the Jewelry Exchange on Forty-seventh Street. She has to figure out how to carry on a business without its heart, what to tell the customers who once knew Mr. Taitz, and how to close it all down. She will mind the store for the next year or so, then, at last, retire from midtown Manhattan.

My brother and I stay with my father. Manny has come to New York from Los Angeles, where he has now been living for decades. Tan and prosperous (he wears a fine Rolex), he pulls a chair up to my Simon's hospice bed. His body is vigorous and strong next to his sick father's.

"Why don't you take five," he says to me. "You look exhausted."

I leave the room and wander the halls. Dying people are everywhere, all thin and twisted, their faces pure as babies'.

Having been there for several weeks, I am growing used to this odd place, this concentration camp of sorts, where the world of the dying literally separates from life and into a spiritual concentrate. There is a holiness here, a privileged beauty. It is the kind of humble wisdom, in time, to which we all come.

In one of the common rooms, relatives play cards or watch TV shows that seem out of place in this land of silence. The floor of this room is beige linoleum, with beige walls to match, like my childhood home. There is one picture of the seashore, and a dirty window. I look through the panes at the faraway sky, wondering if that clear, pale blue light indicates where my father will soon be going. How can sick people take the trip from this world to the next when they are not even feeling well enough to get out of bed? Are their souls young and light and happy? That would be just. That would be fair. That would make sense, after all the weight of painful existence.

I return to the room to find my brother sitting with his head in his hands. He does not look up as I enter.

"Are you okay?"

"He's gone," says Manny, not looking at me.

"What do you mean?"

"Daddy's dead."

Even though my father has been dying for months, this comment seems outlandish. There is no apparent change in my father's appearance.

"No, no, that's how he always looks," I say, explaining all that I know so far. My brother has only recently arrived; he has no idea that hospice patients can look dead for weeks, months sometimes, before they actually go. I have grown used to this nightmare; I could go on like this forever. In fact, to me it no longer seems so bad; the atmosphere among the dying and the nurses is more full of tenderness than the tough world outside. And the sky is really so thin and far away. Let them all rest here a little longer.

"Check his breath," says my brother. "He's not breathing."

I walk briskly over to my father and lean over him. His powerful chest seems to be moving up and down. It takes a while for me to realize that I am the one who is moving. I am shaking, I am crying, my face is near his, and my arms are around him. I am feeling only the ticking pulse of life in myself, and I still want to give it all to him.

I used to think that when my parents died, so would I. After all, they were like my children, my *kinderlach*. Who can live without their *kinderlach*? It was my job to restore their lives, to make everything good again, to give them hope.

I try to calm down enough to see who is breathing: He or I? My body is shaking, my heart is pounding, but he is still. My father's struggles are over. He is really gone from this world.

Right now, all I can do is try to make his poor departing soul feel better.

"You were my hero," I say, weeping over him, hugging his thin body. "You've overcome so much. Thank you for everything. Thank you for giving me your strength."

Manny waits until I am standing up again, until I am upright and wiping my eyes.

"You want to hear something amazing?"

"Okay," I say, sniffling. My hand is still touching my father, as though to keep him in the conversation. One of my brother's hands is touching him, too. If only the right electricity could pass through his two children, my father could come alive again. But we are there; we are alive, and between us, we have given him five grandchildren.

"I was talking to Daddy when you were out of the room.

I told him I was sorry for disappointing him. I asked him to forgive me for, I don't know, being such a tough, challenging kid to raise. You were always more what he wanted."

"You asked him to forgive *you?*"

I thought about all the times my father had struck this boy, this child, my brother. If there was one thing death was good for, it was for enlarging people's emotional capacities.

"And Daddy started waving his hand, back and forth, as though to say, 'Nothing to forgive.'"

"Both his hands? Like fixing watches?"

"Just one hand, like saying, 'Don't worry.'"

He demonstrated the gesture.

"Wow."

"And then he opened his eyes really wide. He looked at me, almost like a kid seeing the world for the first time. Remember, his father was killed when he was just a baby. He didn't know how to be a father, really, a father to a son."

I nodded.

"We looked into each other's eyes," continued my brother, "and there was nothing but love there. And then he took my hand and kissed it, three times. He said to me, 'I love you.'"

And then, my brother continued, almost unable to say the words.

"I actually felt Daddy's soul leave his body and rise up. It was a feeling you get when someone you love steps into the room. You don't have to look. You know they're there. You feel them with you."

My father hadn't left his son behind. In the last seconds of the last hour, he had stepped in and healed him.

I was glad Simon Taitz had died with a salved heart, salving a heart.

Her husband of forty-five years is gone, a man she not only lived with, but worked with every day. A man whose lunches (broiled fish, plum tomato, Golden Delicious) she packed into brown paper bags, and whose Nescafé she poured into a tartan thermos. Gita, now in her late seventies, lives alone in Washington Heights. She still climbs the hills up and down the neighborhood on Sundays, shopping for fruits and vegetables from little greengrocers. She still buys fresh, seeded rye from the bakery, sliced for her by a large chrome machine, and wrapped in a wax paper bag. She still buys Linzer tarts and *babkas*, housed in white square boxes tied with peppermint-striped strings.

When my family comes over to see her, she runs down the hallway to greet us, leaving her door wide open. She wears her apron, smiling, beaming, still capable of real joy. If anything, having grandchildren has released a certain grudging part of her. She loves my children without reservation, without self-preservation. As we approach, we all smell her cooking—chicken soup, chopped liver, matzoh balls.

She is ecstatic, running into and out of the kitchen, carrying dishes and watching us eat.

But most of the time she is alone, and many of her friends are old or have moved to Florida. Not only the Riverdale set is gone, but also the loyalists of Washington Heights, who spend more and more months of the year walking the boardwalks and taking in the sun. Though my family lives in Manhattan, it takes a long subway ride or expensive taxi for her to come see us. As they grow, too, our children increasingly have activities of their own on Sundays. Even when Gita comes over (bringing me magazines and bags of cooked food), they are often out playing sports or seeing friends.

"Mom," my brother says, "you need to live closer to your *einiklach*." He uses the Yiddish word for grandchildren. But she knows that although she and her mother traveled side by side, arm in arm, through their lives, she will not suddenly have the same intense relationship with me. She is reluctant to leave the few old friends she still has in the Heights, women who understand her, whom she sits next to in shul even as their population dwindles and is replaced by loud, new Immigrants from Russia.

My brother is worried. He thinks the neighborhood is too dangerous for a "little old lady." He and his family live in a beautiful house in Beverly Hills. Lemon trees blossom in his garden. He drives a serious car with a quiet engine. Manny has heard, over the years, about drug deals in the Heights, muggings, old people thrown to the ground and robbed at gunpoint at the entrance to the subway or in their own lobbies. He hears rumblings from those who have left, mutterings about the changing flavor of the neighborhood—striped convertibles now playing salsa at glass-shaking, deafening levels, horns that blare "La Cucaracha" as they pass. In the park where the few remaining survivors take their Sabbath stroll, extended families set up tables, radios, grills. They roast whole pigs and drink party-colored sodas. They dance in the open air.

This neighborhood, though, and this apartment, have been the core of Gita's life for decades, and it is dear and familiar to her. Hers has never been an upscale life, and neither she nor my father ever cared about their supposed lack of status. Indeed, they liked not showing their money; they liked economizing so that there was money in the bank for a rainy day. They liked having enough money to offer all their grandchildren a Jewish education, as they did, or to feed the hungry, as they did.

Even now, my mother likes knowing that poor immigrants come here for sanctuary; she understands them, with their close ties to lost worlds. She understands the Spanish-speaking grandmas who wear plastic combs in her hair, the little girls who wear swirly polyester dresses and ruffled socks. She loves seeing the big families, all together (she would love to have such a big family, with daughters who never felt they needed to outdo their families with academics or fancy-shmancy jobs in sterile offices). These are her people. She, too, loves to dance, and they, too, know how to choose a good melon in the fruit store. She and they both cover their good sofas with plastic, and love fake flowers (they never die!). And which Jewish woman of a certain age has not been moved by Latin rhythms? Along with her Chopin and her Rachmaninoff, my mother also tinkered around on the piano with passionate melodies like "Besame Mucho," which had always been big in the Borscht Belt.

Still, she listens when Manny begs her, for his sake, to

move to a better location. Her older child, this tall and prosperous son, is now the "man of the family," and she transfers her obedience from my father to him, saying she will do as he asks. He buys her a new place near me, more than a hundred blocks to the south of her former home. It even has a terrace, just like the old place did.

"She's going to love being so much closer to you and the grandkids," he assures me. I have my worries. I cannot replace her lost mother, I cannot replace her lost country, I cannot replace her lost husband, and I cannot replace her neighborhood, Washington Heights, that vanishing echo of a lost Jewish world. After having children, I understand her better. I can finally grasp the value of a good bowl of soup, a sleeping child under a blanket, the warmth of tradition. I can understand the need to take time to drink tea and eat a buttered onion roll.

But now the deed is done, and Gita has been transferred to the Upper West Side. She and I sit in a pastry store on Seventy-second Street, the heart of her new locale. Yes, it is a kosher pastry store, and the Upper West Side, in parts, is something of a shtetl in itself, full as it is of synagogues and Orthodox families promenading in Riverside Park. But many of the mothers have gotten MBA's along with their Mrs's. They and their husbands are doctors and lawyers, not watchmakers, pearl-stringers, and bakers. They have nannies and maids to take care of their kids, and no one here even tries to speak a good and proper Yiddish.

I myself have forgotten most of the words. While I understand my mother, I can no longer converse with her in our "mother language." Down here, it is even hard to find *The Forward*, the Yiddish paper that she and my father have read since they arrived in America. You can occasionally find it only in its new, abridged English translation.

In the pastry shop, Gita and I share an "almond horn," a marzipan-like confection that ends in a crescent of thick chocolate. She drinks a weak tea with milk, and I have a cappuccino. ("This is what you drink? So strong? No wonder you are always nervous!") A woman steps over and interrupts our snack. She is fortyish, American, bright and friendly. She wears a new, expensive perfume, and her hair has artful highlights.

"Hi, Mrs. Taitz! You're the jewelry store lady, right? I was your customer! I bought opera-length pearls from you, for my mother!"

"Oh, yeh?" my mother takes another sip from her tea. "You look familiar, maybe."

"So!" the woman continues. "What are you doing here? Do you live around here? It's nice, right?"

"Yes, now I do, for a few weeks only."

"Where did you live before?"

"Oh," she sighs, "I lived always in Washington Heights, near the Fort Tryon Park, the Cloisters. But I guess it was a ghetto, like people told me." The word *ghetto* hurts my ears. It is a horrible word for a place she once loved, from which she was uprooted. This move has driven her back into the European past before the American past, and back into her first upheaval. It is the beginning of my mother's going backward.

A few months later, on the children's school break, she travels with us to Barbados. There, under the tropical sun, my mother talks about Nazis and death camps to anyone who will listen—waiters serving fresh mango with mint sprigs, glamorous guests sprawling on chaises, children running to the water slides. She has never avoided telling her stories to us, but now she seems pressed to tell them to as many strangers as possible. It is as though she is running out of time to change the world. To warn it, to wound it. To mark it forever, as she has been marked.

"Would you like some dessert, Madam?" a server might say.

"No, no, I ate good, not like in the camps where we got thin soup so many people starved."

I am perplexed by her inability to relax on the sand, enjoying the blue skies and the Caribbean Sea. I think about my entire life in the shadow of these jarring comments, this indelible, warped perspective. What I don't realize is that a tumor is slowly growing in her brain. As with my father's late rages, which stemmed from a brain metastasis, normal and abnormal are so hard to tell apart.

When we return from Barbados, my mother brightens. Now that my father is gone, she tells me, and she doesn't have to cook or clean, wash his shirts, or run errands at the Exchange, she will take courses in women's studies at a nearby college. She asks me, as she and my father so often did, to help her with the paperwork.

"Take a pen," she says, "and let's write something."

We sit with our heads together and I fill in the information that the college requires. I ask her which courses she wants to take.

"Give me the ones that explain what it means to be a woman."

"Oh, Mommy, you know better than anyone."

At this point, I am also a mother with children—and I wish I could do it half as well as she did. I am only beginning to appreciate what it takes to keep a warm family together, clean and fed.

"No, Sonialeh, I need to learn more. I want to know things like you do. I want to be smart like you."

She says it now without irony, her admiration unmarred by envy or resentment, stroking my free hand as I fill in the forms. With my father gone, we are no longer rivals, but sisters.

"I'm sorry I tore up Paul's letters to you," she tells me another day. "You were about to marry Dan, and I wanted you to be happy, and—and I made a mistake and I hurt you. You married the wrong person and had to get a divorce and even a *get*," she says, referring to the Orthodox Jewish divorce that required three bearded rabbis to stare down at me with great disapproval.

"My poor Sonialeh, I injured you," she concludes humbly.

"It's okay. I'm happy now."

"You had four years between your first marriage and your second. I cost you so much time."

She had always been sad to have lost years in the war, always thinking she had married "late." By the time I married Paul, I was thirty-one.

"It was so long ago. Everything is good now. Who knows what would have happened otherwise? And now we have Emma, Gabriel, and Phoebe."

A few weeks later, on a Sunday, she forgets to call me. Sunday—the day she always visited her grandchildren, arms laden with food and toys. That's all it takes, and I know something is wrong with her. Remorsefully, I think about how often I'd scolded her because the cheap toys, bought on a sidewalk, would break, or because I was cooking organic mashed yams or some other dreary supermom concoction, and she was giving my thrilled children potato chips, cola, and lollipops.

Now, all that, I fear, is over. The peppy, sometimes peppery grandma we knew is gone. For the first time in her life, my industrious mother has started sleeping during the day. When I call to ask when she is coming over, she says she is a little tired, and lets the phone clatter down.

When I call her, the next day, she says, apologetically:

"I think there is something a little wrong with me."

We go to the hospital where my father's tumor was discovered, and wait on the same floor, deep in the basement, for tests. We are there for hours, in a cold limbo with glossy, gray-painted walls and floors, evoking the feeling of hopelessness. By the end of the day, we have the death sentence: My mother has a glioblastoma multiforme. A deadly and incurable brain cancer, large as a lemon and inoperable. Of course, my "research" soon informs me that some have had the operation, and that it has bought them more time. I track down the best neurosurgeon in the hospital and tell him that Ms. Taitz is a concert-level pianist who survived the Holocaust. I tell him that her grandchildren need her. Surprisingly, my words cause him to rush to her room.

After reviewing her chart, he realizes he cannot help. The tumor crosses the corpus callosum, he explains, taking me outside. This is the vital tissue that connects left brain to right. Operating on it would make the rest of her life totally miserable.

"My dear lady," he says, leaning over her hospital bed and taking her soft, strong fingers in his, "I wish I could do more for you."

She answers, "Oh, you are very nice."

After he leaves, she starts crying, and then, suddenly, she

looks at me intently and says: "I am so sorry to leave you, So-nialeh, a mother with three small children. But at least they are not babies anymore. And you are strong."

My oldest is now nine, the middle one seven, and the "baby" almost four, the age I was when I entered the hospital asking for my box of sixty-four colors. Unlike me, these children are happy, engaged, alert; they not only have their jumbo boxes of Crayolas, but tempera paints; Play-Doh kits; dolls, pocket-sized and large, that talk sensibly and hold down jobs; and magical cities, often mechanized, made of limitless amounts of Lego. But now, despite all my care, they will be bereft of a Bubbe who burbles to them in Yiddish about how much she loves them. Gita is irreplaceable, to them and to me. There will be no more Simons or Gitas in this world, ever.

"You're not leaving us," I say, trying to comfort her, trying to convince myself.

"Okay," she answers agreeably.

"We'll figure something out," I say. But this time, I am not so sure.

A Life

For the last time, my mother tells me how she and her mother survived the war. It is, of course, a story she has told me since I was born. But now it is as though she is passing the story over to me, and for all the times I have heard it before, it sounds as though it now contains a secret meaning that, perhaps one day, I will understand.

"My mother and I were still surviving, at the end of the war," she says. "We had spent so much time digging trenches in the cold, almost giving up, but we had survived.

"And now, the Russians were coming, and the Germans were fleeing. They were trying to hide all the evidence, and kill all the witnesses. So before they could leave us poor women behind, they decided to finish with us.

"From bunker to bunker, they came in, with needles, shots, filled with gasoline. They were giving injections to the women in their veins with this poison that burned them. When they ran out of the gasoline, they used only air; that also killed them. I heard the poor women screaming in pain. I knew they were being killed and losing their lifes."

My mother used that word often. *Lifes.* Whenever she said or wrote the word *alive,* she gave it, perhaps inadvertently, an extra meaning with her version of it: "a life."

"My mother and I didn't know what to do. The Nazis were rushing from bunker to bunker. Finally, I said to your Bubbe—let's run, Mama, let's run quickly to one of the bunkers where already they killed everyone there.

"I knew it was risking our lifes but there was no other choice. It was nighttime, it was dark. So I grabbed my mama and we ran. I pulled her so we could go fast into one of the bunkers where the women were dying. There were many lying dead already. We lay next to these poor women, we stayed there, we lay quiet.

"And then, after many hours, the morning came. We heard voices shouting:

"Come out! It is over! You are free!'

"We were a life, Sonia, among all the poor dead. We were a life."

Now, I take my mother home and try to keep her alive. She is, truly, "a life," always capable of joy and laughter. For as long as I have known her, she has hummed as she cooked and cleaned. And now, despite her tumor, she still hums and cooks and cleans. (Her favorite, for some reason, is now "Cielito Lindo.")

I think about how my parents have always kept themselves useful and busy. Both parents, he with his watchmaking hands, rising above him in his deathbed, she with her happy, constructive housewifery. Always making something, going for something, accomplishing something, from returning a dead wristwatch to life (and strapping it onto the hand of a grateful owner) to seeing to it that everyone was fed, wore fresh clothes, and slept on clean, soft sheets.

I, on the other hand, am more and more like that "lovely, dark and deep" forest that Robert Frost wistfully regarded. The "promises" I have had to keep have faded away; they seem intense and silly. Yale. The Jewish people. Fight this, sustain that. Shoulder the burden of memory. Increasingly, since marrying Paul, I have come to live in the world of moments, moods, and colors. I read, I write, I even publish, but mostly, I tend to my children. When I am sad, I wallow deep in some primordial bog that is hard to escape. The fight has gone out of me, and the roiling ambition. Instead of grabbing diplomas or wearing power suits, I crave cuddles with my children and pets; I wear yoga pants and T-shirts.

My mother, at seventy-six and with a tumor in her head, still dresses in pretty floral frocks; she wears hose and cherry-red lipstick. She still bakes more honey cakes on Rosh Hashanah week than I have ever done in my life. Joyfully, her fingers fly over the keyboard, when I have long forgotten my greatest musical accomplishment—the "Für Elise." The gorgeous, passionate music of her life envelops me. It is heard only by me, her daughter, and not a concert hall full of applauders. I appreciate her more and more as a person, as a woman and as an artist. As Thomas Gray said in his "Elegy Written in a Country Churchyard": "Full many a flower is born to blush unseen/And waste its sweetness on the desert air."

Gita's sweetness is no longer wasted on me.

But this cancer is deadly and the prognosis horrifyingly bad. As with my father, the possibility of her dying of a horrible illness after all she's been through seems obscene to me. Don't such people deserve to die peacefully in their beds at the age of one hundred? Again, I run around trying to make that possible. The thought of my father's last days and months, the anger and sense of betrayal, haunt me. I felt his Holocaust in those last days when, chained to the bed, he ranted and fought his fate. Though I was his "special girl," his chosen of the chosen of the chosen, I did not save him. What, then, was I born for?

I will save my mother. I will perpetuate this cute Jewish grandma in my children's lives, and they will appreciate her as I never did, as I am just beginning to. For being, simply, "a life." A sweet and modest life.

Over the next few months, I find experimental treatments, torturous attempts at hope. Fortunately for her, I eschew the goat trachea and mitaki mushroom route. Instead, I discover an experimental treatment protocol in her hospital. It involves thalidomide, that awful drug that, decades ago, caused babies to be born with rudimentary limbs. The theory is that this drug is an anti-angiogenic—it stops blood cells from replicating, and hence kills off tissue—hopefully, in my mother's case, cancerous tissue. I fight to make sure she is entered into the experiments, even though technically her tumor is too large. I plead and beg to put her on the line for life. And she does enter the experiment.

The tumor shrinks. Scans show that it has gone from lemon to olive. Gita stops talking about ghettos and holocausts, and, though weak, is as happy as I have ever seen her. She looks at me with pure love now. She offers no advice, no criticisms. She enjoys her food, the weather, flowers in a vase. She continues to play Chopin flawlessly. Like my father's hands, hers remember, and they enter the soul of this rich music.

It is early afternoon on a cozy winter's day. Gita is in bed, and I am at her side, when she looks at me and says, emphatically:

"Sonialeh: Du hast nicht keine shlechte bein . . . "

I am massaging her limbs with her favorite almond-scented cream, and my hands stop. Did she really say that? The words she said, they mean: You do not have one mean bone.

Has she forgotten how mean I have been, so arrogant, such a snob, thinking that I, with my fancy diplomas, was superior to anything she could ever achieve? Has she forgiven me for even daring to accept my father's praise, conditional praise, which should have all, unconditionally, been given to her?

A terrible memory floods my heart at this moment of forgiveness.

When I first returned to law school after Oxford, I'd rented a small apartment near campus. My mother had called to see how I was getting along, and I complained about how filthy the place was. In frustration, I mentioned that I needed to go to a cocktail gathering for new and returning students. What if I never got the apartment clean in time for the party?

The law school get-together was to be held in a festive little grass area between grand gothic buildings. In the end, I was able to go, able to relax in my sorbet-colored sundress and pretty cardigan, and toss my hair. I was able to live it up, because my mother had come up to New Haven, and was cleaning my filthy apartment. Gita had insisted. She had hung up the phone and run to Grand Central Terminal in an ecstasy of being needed, after so long, by her daughter.

It was all, of course, perverse and painful, unnatural and wrong. There I was, having a good time meeting the faculty at a garden party. There was good champagne; there were cunning little sandwiches. My high-heeled sandals made divots in the lawn, and if ever I wobbled, a strong, blazer-wearing male arm was there to gallantly catch me. We all exchanged witticisms—legal, intellectual, literary bon mots. Oxford had given me polish and veneer, and I felt cool and confident. As the sun set and the air chilled, I began to feel relief about coming back to law school. This circle of practical wisdom could shelter me for the next two years. All I had to do was study. Perhaps I could even meet someone new here, someone whose parents did not fear a smart, ambitious Jewish lady. A sterling career was open to me again. Maybe I could even find time to write.

When I returned to my apartment, laughter and chatter rang in my ears. I looked forward to sharing my good mood with my mother. But when I opened the door, everything vanished. There she was, my mother, crouched in the dark, scrubbing at the floor with a brush, like a mythical slave.

"Why are you in the dark, Mommy?"

It was like some kind of sad Jewish joke. How many Jewish mothers does it take to screw in a light bulb? None! Thank you, don't worry about me. I'll just sit in the dark. I'll just clean your mess in the black world you threw me into.

"Your light went out, I don't know what happened." Her voice was exhausted, accusing. "It's broken," she said. "And I can't find new bulbs. I can't find anything in this dark place of yours."

"Oh, Mommy," I said, running to the kitchen to find a fresh bulb for the overhead fixture and get her some water. My mother was covered in sweat. There was no air conditioner, and though it had been cool in the courtyard, my new apartment now seemed suffocating.

"So, Sonia," she said, taking a long drink. Her eyes sized me up in my pretty dress and sandals.

"Did you have a nice time at your party?"

"Yes," I admitted, crying, hugging her. "I did."

Now, as I sit before her, rubbing her work-worn fingers with cream, can she see how my heart broke—as hers must have—that evening? My mother was a concert-level pianist. She could have been famous—a champagne drinker in privileged stone courtyards—were it not for the war. My father and I often reduced her to what she called "a Nothing"—a terminal designation she refused to accept. But even if all she was was a jeweler's helper, someone who sold solitaires, tied ribbons, ran errands, and sometimes strung pearls, even if all she was was a mother, a mopper, a soup-kitchen slave, she was worth ten of me. Can it be that she forgives me for not seeing this before? For thinking she was any less "special" than my father?

It is clear that she does forgive me. She has always known how to live, and even now, she seems to know how to cherish each moment. Few remain, and yet she enjoys them. She is the parent who will teach me to surrender to love, however battle-torn and damaged, and what it is to die with grace. Without saying the words, we both know that her diagnosis is terminal, and that the end can only be postponed for precious days like this one.

My mother's eyes are calm with love as I rub her hands, lingering over each finger. She gives her floor-scrubbing, music-making hands to me, and I soothe them. They soothe me.

Speedo

WHEN SHE DIES, Gita is wearing a pretty pink night-gown and white Speedo sweat socks. Looking at her feet, I see her as someone who was always ready to run and do some "menial," essential task for someone else. And now her feet have come to a rest, and I remember how many times I'd seen those white socks on them.

There were Speedos on her feet when we watched *Peyton Place* on her bed, or read *Modern Screen* together. She always told me that my feet looked like hers, both small with high arches. She wanted me to be like her; this small area of con-sonance gave her comfort.

"Look," I said one day, trying to amplify the bonding. "Look at my second toe, exactly the same length as the first, right?"

"Right," she said agreeably. "Just like me."

Lying on a flowery bedspread, we created a game in which our feet moved together in rhythm, left and right like windshield wipers. I'd talk to her feet, and they'd answer: a "nod" for yes, side-to-side for no.

"Do you like Rodney Harrington?" I'd ask about the tawny-haired all-American boy of the miniseries.

Her feet would nod, "yes, yes."

"Do you like the girl, Allison?" she'd ask my feet, referring to the frail blonde heroine of the program.

"Mm hmm," my feet would say.

"Ask me if I like Betty!" I'd urge. Betty was the dark-haired bad girl; she was the one with the past.

"Do you like the spicy girl, Betty?"

Here my heels would kick the mattress with vigor, and my mother would laugh. It was spicy people who kept us rapt. Then the commercial would end, and we'd watch again, our feet still.

Gita played this "footsie" game happily, throughout my childhood. Inside the socks, her feet were like stuffed toys to me, hand puppets, pets, and friends.

On Sundays she'd put on Speedo socks when she'd come to my house, taking off her hose and her heels to clean up the children's toys, or rush to a high chair and take over a feeding. *She* was Speedo, and running to help was her essence, rushing to visit us, rushing to her own door to stand in the hallway when we all came to visit Grandma and Grandpa in Washington Heights. Running errands for my father at the Jewelry Exchange. Ready to grab another dish from the stove and race it to the table. Always ready. *She* was the one who was *tamid muchan*, not me. She was the true warrior, tireless and willing.

On her last day, she is mellow, smiling.

I can see love in her eyes, and I take a chance.

"Who did you really love more? Manny?"

"Yes, he was a boy, and I had lost my father and my two little brothers," she says easily. "And he was always close to me."

Then she adds, "But sometimes, you, more than anyone."

This is even better than my father, who loved me most when I succeeded. The love she holds for me is there, even though I have failed her in every way.

She is so sweet as a dying person; she is so sweet even as she lies dead. So different from my father, who raged until the end, who took dying as a personal and undeserved final insult.

Gita is teaching me something about life that until then, despite all the diplomas, I had not learned. Becoming a mother has brought me close to the secret of her wisdom. Watching her fade, as love burns constant in her heart, brings me even closer. She is a woman, with a woman's modest and forgiving heart. If my father's main question to me was "What did you accomplish?," hers was, "What can I do for you?" or, "Isn't this a joy, sitting here with our glass of tea?" She could always admire a red-and-green McIntosh apple as she wheeled her little shopping cart up and down the streets of upper Broadway, Washington Heights, New York. She was a connoisseur of good produce, and she shared all her bounty.

"A prune danish like this, you can't get in heaven," my mother would say, unwrapping the white wax parcel and biting into bliss. "Take a bite," she'd offer. "Nem doch!" (So take!) "Oy, is it good."

Gita found so much in this world to be good. She loved flowers: pansies and carnations, babies' breath and forget-me-nots. She loved them whether real or silk or plastic, in patterns on her wallpaper, on tablecloths and duvets and housedresses and frocks. Her last bedspread, which Manny has bought her, is a gorgeous blaze of golden sunflowers. It gives her great joy, and she comments on it often.

For the most part, until the end, he is away in California, where he works as a lawyer and real estate developer. I am with her every day. Spooning raspberry ices into her mouth is the last thing I do for my mother. They are the last thing she tastes on this earth. I am glad they are sweet. Soon after, Gita falls into a deep sleep, snoring lightly and unevenly. A visiting nurse has been there for the last few hours, watching game shows in the living room. I go out and ask her to check if my mother is all right. She isn't. The nurse tells me that her blood pressure has gone really low—one precursor of death.

How can she die? I argue, pointlessly. Her tumor has shrunk! She's enjoying her day—what's the rush?

But she can. Gita lies back, a pretty princess with a heart that is hardly beating at all. My little girl, my mother, free of all her worries, work, and sorrows, floats among a field of yellow flowers.

In the ambulance, I lean over her and give her secret chest compressions. (I was always ready for this, learning CPR at the Red Cross on the day my father turned sixty.)

When Gita was first diagnosed, my practical brother asked her to sign a legal document called a DNR. DO NOT RESCUCITATE. He was still reeling from the horrors of my father's lingering cancer death, not long before. "If I ever look like that," he says, "like a living corpse with my mind half gone, please shoot me." I completely understood.

Nonetheless, I am now thinking—DO RESCUCITATE!!

If a desert can bloom, if exiles can return, if an entire people can rise up from ashes and sand, so can she. So can my little Gita. I want her even as she is—she is still our Bubbe, our soft hands, our onions and bay leaves, our story.

But she dies. There is a smile on her face in death, a radiant smile. She looks alive, not like my father, who looked shrunken and dead for weeks in the hospice. She actually looks young and healthy. Her Speedo socks are bright and white on her pretty, small feet. I remember how I used to put my hands on them, lightly, when she'd play the piano, going up and down with them as she pressed on the pedals below.

The hospital lets me stay with her as long as I want, and I stay for hours.

At her funeral, I cry as I have never cried before. I cry for her sad life, and I cry for her sweet girlishness, and her cuteness, and her socks, and the endless chicken soup and kitchen pan bustling . . .

I cry that we were never close enough. That I never learned to cook her recipes—yes, the boiled chicken and the strange cabbage *galuptzie* and the mattress cake. The latter was a pound cake, thick as a tire (you could bend it and not break it) into which my mother spooned canned apricots in a rhythmic pattern that resembled the buttons on an old-fashioned mattress. I never learned to make that cake, chopped liver, flanken, or matzoh balls. All I can do is order in, and I blame feminism for that, for my contempt for her thankless domestic sacrifices. I am thanking her now as my children and I begin to try her old recipes.

They praise Mother Theresa for devoting her life to others, so why not Gita Taitz? The soup for housebound Mrs. Schroodel, the packages of warm clothes for relatives stuck in Siberia, the fish sandwiches in onion rolls for my father, and the spaghetti and ketchup for my brother and me. The hems she sewed, putting a thread in my mouth for good luck as her needle flew. Her housework, mopping the floor of her tiny kitchen, hauling a vacuum around our thick, brownish-gold carpeting. The beds she made, layer upon layer of flower-patterned sheets, blankets and duvets of cozy polyester batting.

My mother, whether or not she understood me, would have died for me. When the Nazis put her mother on the "death" line, my mother ran over to her side and somehow got her out. She could have been shot, but she didn't care. Had God asked her to take her child to a mountain and sacrifice her, Gita Taitz, unlike Abraham, would not have obeyed. She would have said, "Take me instead." She would have run up the mountain and laid herself down on the altar for me, as she once did for her mother. That is what a real mother can do.

And here is her last gift to a difficult child:

"Du hast nicht keine shlechte bein . . . "
You don't have a mean bone.

These final words are beautiful, and they will have to suffice me for the rest of my life. Coming from her, they mean more than Yale and Oxford put together. Like my dream of the magic mirror in *Romper Room*, Gita finally sees me through the glass. And I see her through mine. Even in her death, she is sweet, without specialness, or seeking specialness. She is mother, fragrant, giving.

I am not only the watchmaker's daughter; I am hers.

Acknowledgments

I'D LIKE TO THANK my parents, Simon and Gita Taitz, to whom this book is a love letter and tribute. I'd also like to thank my big brother, Emanuel, who not only urged me to have my say but reminded me that when our father faced obstacles, he'd gather the will to "walk through walls." With Emanuel's encouragement, I have "walked through walls" to bring this memoir to light, and would have given up trying long before had my brother not kept me brave. His gift to the world of two wonderful daughters, Jennifer and Michelle, is also a source of great joy to me, as it was to our parents.

I owe a deep debt of gratitude, again, to Ellie McGrath, my wonderful, gracious publisher, and her husband, Paul Witteman (the "Wit" of McWitty); Abby Kagan, for her beautiful design and enormous heart; and Jenny Carrow, for the striking cover, which reflects compassion and inspired understanding. Lynn Auld Schwarz, you are the most precious friend, reader, and supporter; I am also grateful to Debra Berman, Wendy Durica, Jan Olofsen, Bonni-Dara

Michaels, Kelly Kaminski, Susan Weinstein, Tamar Yellin, Alyssa Quint, Geraldine Baum, Professor Henry Feingold, and Tammy Williams, gorgeous, gracious, and good.

Dearest John Patrick Shanley: You took me under your wing, let me hoist your Oscar, poured me Sauternes (in Washington Heights, no less), and shared your agent with me. I'm not forgetting that.

Jacques Sebisaho: Your life as a survivor of African genocide, the good works you do, and the beauty and health of your wife, Mimy Mudekeraza, and children—all are an inspiration to me.

Thank you to Lawrence Van Gelder of *The New York Times*, for first putting me into the spotlight, and to Lucinda Blumenfeld, for keeping me there.

Denise Shannon, I owe you a great debt for your unshakable belief in this book. I hope I've made you proud.

Lastly, to Paul and to our children, Emma, Gabriel, and Phoebe, with thanks for sorrows divided and joys multiplied.

About the Author

SONIA TAITZ is an essayist, playwright, and the critically acclaimed author of *In the King's Arms* and *Mothering Heights*. Her writing has been featured in *The New York Times*, *The New York Observer*, *O: The Oprah Magazine*, *More*, and *Psychology Today*, where she is a columnist on family trauma. She has been cited on ABC's *Nightline*, in a PBS special on love, and in countless quotation anthologies.

Sonia Taitz earned a JD from Yale Law School; she has served as Law Guardian for foster children and an ER advocate for victims of rape and domestic violence. She also holds an MPhil in nineteenth-century English literature from Oxford University, where she was awarded the Lord Bullock Prize for her fiction. She lives in New York City.